When You're Feeling Lonely

Finding a Way Out

Charles Durham

InterVarsity Press
Downers Grove
Illinois 60515

InterVarsity Press is the book-publishing division of Inter-Varsity Christian Fellowship, a student movement active on campus at hundreds of universities, colleges and schools of nursing. For information about local and regional activities, write IVCF, 233 Langdon St., Madison, WI 53703.

Distributed in Canada through InterVarsity Press, 860 Denison St., Unit 3, Markham, Ontario L3R 4H1, Canada.

Acknowledgment is made to the following for permission to reprint copyrighted material:

All Scripture quotations, unless otherwise indicated, are from the Revised Standard Version of the Bible, copyrighted 1946, 1952, © 1971, 1973.

The poem on page 34 is an excerpt from "The Creation" from God's Trombones by James Weldon Johnson. Copyright 1927 by the Viking Press Inc. Copyright renewed 1955 by Grace Nail Johnson. Reprinted by permission of Viking Penguin Inc.

The poem, "Meeting," on page 83 is taken from Poems by Boris Pasternak, translated by Eugene M. Kayden, © 1963. Used by permission of the University of Colorado Board of Regents.

Cover photograph: David Singer

ISBN 0-87784-915-3

Printed in the United States of America

Library of Congress Cataloging in Publication Data
Durham, Charles, 1939-
   When you're feeling lonely.

   Includes bibliographical references.
   1. Loneliness–Religious aspects–Christianity.
I. Title.   II. Title: When you are feeling lonely.
BV4911.D87   1984   248.8'6   84-10499
ISBN 0-87784-915-3

16	15	14	13	12	11	10	9	8	7	6	5	4	3	2	1
97	96	95	94	93	92	91	90	89	88	87	86	85	84		

For Linda, my wife.
And for Mark, David, Deborah, and Rebekah,
my children.

Preface

A few weeks ago my eight-year-old daughter said to her mother, "Dad's just wasting his time writing a book about loneliness!"

Linda asked Rebekah, "What makes you think he's wasting his time?"

" 'Cause, Mom. Nobody will buy it, 'cause nobody's lonely."

"Nobody's lonely?"

"Nobody! I don't know a single person who is!"

Rebekah, I wish you were right. But I'm afraid the warm view from your little girl's heart has misled you. There are a great many lonely people in this world, and though you don't realize it just yet, you do know some of them. It's just that they keep their hurt so well hidden.

I've written about loneliness because I believe it's such a big problem to folk everywhere. Of course, I hope that you are never lonely. But if you ever are, maybe this book will be a help to you.

Even if God blesses you with a life full of those you love and who love you in return, you will meet some very lonely people. And when you do, maybe the things you learned from this book will help you know how to reach out and help take their loneliness away.

Part One
Loneliness

1

What Is Loneliness?

"Loneliness is the first thing
which God's eye named not good."
John Milton

IN THE WINTER OF 1934, Navy Admiral Richard Byrd lived for five months in a buried shack on the Ross Ice Barrier near the South Pole. The most honored explorer of his time, Byrd had come to collect weather data from that formidable environment. No man had ever ventured so far to the south to remain so long and lived, for on the surface of the Ross Ice Barrier is "the coldest cold on the face of the earth."

The obstacles to his mission's success were great. First there was the cold, as low as eighty-three degrees below zero. There were the mountains of powdery, moving snow that threatened to trap him in his hovel. The terrain was a sheet of ice thousands of feet thick, and as level and featureless as the top of a table. And there was the darkness. In mid-April the sun dipped below the horizon and did not return. By mid-May the only sunlight was a brief reddish glow low in the northern sky each day at noon. All was "one layer of darkness piled on top of the other."

Byrd suffered from frostbite, stings from wind-blown pellets of sleet, monoxide poisoning, lack of sleep and malnutrition. He was lost in a blizzard during a foray from his shelter and was once nearly swallowed up in a crevasse.

Yet, when he returned to civilization and wrote an account of his experience on the Barrier, the title of his account did not emphasize the terrain, the weather, the sickness, the danger, or the darkness. Rather it emphasized the most fearfully devastating part of the entire winter. He called his book simply *Alone*.[1] Neither the winds, the great dunes of snow, the nausea nor the long, dense night could compare with the horror of being isolated from fellow human beings.

A Universal Problem
Though we may never have experienced isolation to the degree that Byrd did, we all know something of what it means to be alone. The fact that you are reading this book indicates that you are concerned in some way about the universal problem of loneliness, because either you or someone about whom you care is lonely.

Station in life does not immunize us to the experience. Having money does not prevent it. Being married is not a guarantee against it, nor is parenthood, nor accomplishment, nor a winning face or personality.

Defined by experience, loneliness is having just said good-by to your oldest son as he leaves home to work in a far-off city. It is putting one plate of bacon and eggs on a table that is bare for want of a woman's touch. Loneliness is coming home in the evening to open the door on a still and empty house. Loneliness in twentieth-century America is living a thousand miles from the community where you grew up, a thousand miles from favorite places, from parents and friends who love you. Loneliness is having a spouse who is married to work, or one who believes the marriage vows were a mistake. It's not knowing which parent to live with after the divorce. It's moving to a new suburb and finding nothing in common with any of your neighbors, finding that you are the only person on your block who works at home, and that there's no church of your denomination within fifty miles.

Loneliness is being the only fourth-grader in the room who cannot work the math problem. It's having broken the law and being shut away from your family; and it's being the family whose loved one is shut away. It is also being forty years old, desperately wanting a home and family, but having no spouse. Or it's having a spouse who can't stand children. It is having lived for fifty years in a house you have grown to love, and then being forced to find a new community when it is demolished by urban renewal. It's being in a retirement home, seeing only the aides who are too busy for a warm, lingering touch. It's having lost your mate of forty years, and having no children. To be lonely is to have just been asked for a divorce.

Loneliness is a painful state of mind, a feeling deep in the pit of your stomach. It may be mildly irritating or totally incapacitating. It is very near the top of that list of things we fear most.

One survey revealed that one of every four respondents said they had been lonely within the preceding few weeks, and one out of nine reported severe loneliness in the week immediately past. Women, married or unmarried, admit to more loneliness than men. Severe loneliness is prevalent among the unmarried of both sexes. And among those who have lost a mate in death it is reported to be the most serious of all problems.[2] It is likely to be found among the recently divorced, those who have lost their jobs, or those who have moved to a new community. It is found among teen-agers, the old, the handicapped, and minority groups.

Loneliness is more of a problem in America today than it was one hundred years ago. Social scientists blame the breakdown of the nuclear and extended family as well as changing behavioral standards and the fact that one in five Americans moves in any given year. They have concluded that we are not nearly so adaptable to this kind of change as we had thought, and that the price in loneliness is very high.

But What Is Loneliness?

Though we are able to define loneliness by using examples, and though most of us have been lonely at one time or another, we would find it difficult to offer a dictionary definition of the term. We might say that it is "an empty feeling." Yet it is obviously more complicated than that. In the rest of this chapter we will attempt to analyze loneliness and come up with a workable definition.

First, it is important to see that loneliness is not the same thing as being alone. There are many who live alone and are quite content to do so. There are others who live with a mate and several children, and yet are lonely. So we may say that though being alone makes it more likely that we will feel lonely, loneliness is not a particular situation, but rather a state of mind.

It is possible to be lonely with others around us because our inner needs are not being met. For example, I may feel that no one understands me, or that my mate disapproves of me, or that others do not sympathize with some view of life which is very important to me. There may be things that I crave to share with another, and yet no one wishes to share them with me. So though others surround me, I may still feel alone.

This leads us closer to a definition. We can say that loneliness is pain caused by some sort of isolation from a person or persons. This isolation may be physical, ideological or emotional.

Can Christians Be Lonely?

Some say that loneliness is an illness. Others say that it is an expression of self-centeredness. And there are more than a few who say that it results from the lack of a right relationship with God or from a failure to trust him enough. Some even say that loneliness is sin. Yet I know folk who are balanced, unselfish, deeply committed and trusting Christians who have bouts with loneliness. Missionaries suffer because of the great distance between themselves and their families. Any Christian who takes an unpopular stand is likely to feel isolated from others. We can sense the pain in Paul's words when he says, "No one took my part; all deserted me" (2 Tim 4:16), and in David's bitter soliloquy when he reflected, "I am like a vulture of the wilderness, like an owl of the waste places; I lie awake, I am like a lonely bird on the housetop" (Ps 102: 6-7). It has been said that these men felt as they did because they were not trusting God at the moment. But that view seems unrealistic and without scriptural support.

When I was a child we sang a gospel chorus that claimed that once Jesus came into your heart you would "never be lonely again." The song ridiculed loneliness as a foolish, un-Christian feeling. I believe this is a mistake. As we will see in the next chapter, loneliness is a form of temptation, and it is possible to luxuriate in self-pity because of a sense of isolation, but the feelings themselves are not sinful.

John Milton said, "Loneliness is the first thing which God's eye named not good." Of course Milton was referring to Genesis 2:18, "Then the LORD God said, 'It is not good that the man should be alone.' "

Now I'm amazed by that for these reasons. First, man was not yet fallen, sin had not spoiled the scene, yet God said something was missing. Something "not good," yet not diabolic, was present in the Garden. And I am amazed because God and man were in perfect fellowship, yet man lacked something important! With our usual simplistic approach, both of these facts seem out of place, yet there they are: something not good before the Fall, and a lack in spite of the full, unhindered presence of God.

This poses a problem for us. How can man have God in his fullness, and yet lack something? I think the answer is quite simple. God made man with a built-in need for two kinds of companionship: companionship with himself, and companionship with other human beings. French mathematician and philosopher Blaise Pascal is believed to have said that in every human heart there is a God-shaped vacuum. But I am convinced that there is also a "human-shaped vacuum," a need for fellow human beings, placed there by God, and intended by him to be filled only by others of Adam's kind. He made it so at the beginning, and until Eve was created the need was not filled. The lack was "not good." This thought is basic to all that follows in this book: loneliness is essentially not good.

Three Lessons
If this is so, then at least three lessons logically follow. First, loneliness is not sin. It is neither selfishness nor lack of trust. Rather, it is a symptom that points to a need. Just as pain indicates that something is wrong with one's body, so a feeling of loneliness indicates that something is lacking or twisted in our personal relationships.

The need to which this pain points may be for a relationship with God through Jesus Christ, or for repair of an existing but damaged relationship with God. Or the pain may point to a need for another human being.

Dr. Robert Weiss, a respected social scientist, calls loneliness "a deficit condition, a response to the absence of specific relational provisions."[3] He is saying that we have needs for relationships with others; that there are provisions for meeting those needs; that if they are not met there is a lack, a deficit, that makes us feel lonely. This analysis agrees quite well with Genesis 2:18.

The second lesson is that loneliness is not a condition which we should seek. It is not healthy to be without companionship for great periods of time. Yet, some people think isolation is an honorable state of painful grandeur. Some use it to shield themselves from the risks of social relationships. But nothing of lasting good is produced by shunning others as a way of life. Of course there are times when we should seek as Jesus did to be alone to pray, study or think. But those planned periods of isolation do not produce loneliness.

A third lesson from Genesis 2:18 is seen in what God did to meet Adam's need. When the proper time came, God supplied the missing element. He created another person to fill the vacuum which he had created in Adam. He gave Eve a similar need, and Adam was the person to meet her need. When we recognize that we are lonely, we should ask why. What relationship or relationships are lacking or need to be repaired? Only after identifying the deficit can we correct it.

Different Kinds of Loneliness
Loneliness is not all of one kind. Already we have divided our need for relationships into two kinds, a need for God and a need for other human beings. I believe that a desire to know God exists in all people of every race, culture and community.

The need for other human beings is self-evident. But we don't long for just anyone; we long for particular types of human relationships. First, we need the family. This is the most basic of all institutions. Some say that the family will someday cease to exist. I don't believe that. It appears to me that the family is so basic, filling so many needs, that if it did not exist already humanity would invent it. And once having invented it, we would prize it as the greatest discovery ever made.

When I say *family* I mean the immediate family composed of parents, brothers and sisters, wife and children; and I mean also the extended family: grandparents, aunts, uncles and cousins. If we are isolated from the family either geographically or emotionally, certain needs are likely to go unmet.

Our second need is for a mate. This is a general statement that has some exceptions. But on the whole each person has a drive toward intimacy with one of the opposite sex. Deprived of this, we are likely to experience loneliness.

Third, we have a need for a few close friends. Normally, for practical reasons, these friends are of our own sex. They meet needs for confidentiality, emotional support, counsel and loyalty. Without them there is a void. If we have never had such friends, we may not feel the absence very deeply, but having had one and lost him or her, we grieve as though we had lost a member of the family.

Last of all, we need a social network. This network is composed of many casual friends with whom we share interests, activities or simply the area in which we live. Some common element brings us together: a political interest, our occupation, the church, a hobby, yard work, children.

There is nothing quite like a good community to make us feel warm inside. My wife, Linda, and I have lived in the same community for eleven years. When we came to this small western Kansas town my work threw me into contact with many people from all segments of the population, from the poor to the wealthy. I cannot express how satisfying it is to be able to walk into almost any store in town and be greeted by name. We know many of the teachers and school administrators, folk in the town government, ministers, doctors, other laborers, the people who own and operate the newspaper. A couple of years ago I had an accident that put me in the hospital for three days. I was cared for by a doctor I had met many times in other circumstances, by nurses who have children in school with mine, and by other staff and technicians with whom I am personally acquainted. I had many visits from friends. All of these things took away the usual stress and isolation of illness.

Without this network of casual friends, many people become profoundly lonely and life loses much of its positive quality. It would be almost impossible to overemphasize the wonderful warmth of being part of a community. I am not suggesting that this kind of community is easily available to all, but its benefits are so great that they are worth every possible effort we can put forth to become part of one.

In our society, a wife who does not work outside the home and who moves into a new and perhaps incompatible neighborhood may suffer most from a lack of community. Without the natural support of other women in the community, her husband and children are called on to fill emotional needs that would normally be cared for in other ways. This places abnormal strains on family ties and contributes to trouble in the home, even to its complete breakdown. The value of the community is very great indeed.

No Substitutes, Please

In the chapters that follow, we will discuss each of these needs for relationships in greater detail. But from the beginning we need to observe this fact: *one kind of relationship cannot be substituted for another!* God has made us with great complexity and diversity. Our social needs are not simple. Just as my children cannot take the place of my wife, or vice versa, many good friends cannot take the place of God. Conversely, God does not intend to take the place of human friends, and close family ties do not fill the need for a social network.

This implies that we can be content and happy in one area of our relationships and quite lonely in another.

It is also possible to have others gathered around us and still be lonely. *Emotional isolation* has to do not with whether we have relationships, but with the quality of those we do have. We may be married, living in the same house with our spouse, eating at the same table, sleeping in the same bed and even sharing frequently in sexual embrace, and yet be isolated from each other at the most important level.

I am using the term *emotional isolation* differently from some leading researchers, but this use expresses more clearly what I have in mind than any other term seems to be able to do. We will explore this further in subsequent chapters.

A Wonderful Thing
There is a wonderful thing about loneliness. While it feels very much like depression, it is not quite the same. When we are depressed, and the reason for our depression is removed, some of the psychological and physical changes that have occurred within us linger, and we return to normal rather slowly. But when we are lonely, and the deficit in our relational life is filled, our loneliness vanishes instantly![4]

Patience is needed to find the person or persons, establish the network or change the attitudes that have caused our loneliness, but when we discover the friends we have needed and establish relationships with them, the effects of the problem vanish and we are free. This should be a great encouragement to you if you are suffering from loneliness. Read on with hope!

2

The Dangers of Loneliness

"Loneliness that spreads out
like a desert."
C. S. Lewis, **The Problem of Pain**

WHY DID GOD SAY THAT loneliness is bad? Does it do something to us? Murder takes away life. Is loneliness something like murder? Yes. It is destructive to humanity and poses a great many dangers.

Loneliness Causes Pain
In the first place, loneliness is painful. It hurts. The kind of hurt depends on the kind of problem that creates the loneliness, but hurt it does. Constant pain is debilitating. You probably know someone who is in constant physical pain. No matter how strong that person's character, the pain takes its toll. He or she gradually loses the appearance of youthfulness, wrinkles begin to form, facial skin begins to sag, light goes out of the eyes. The condition is made all the worse because the person is able to reflect on the pain, asking why, wondering if there is a way out, ever looking for escape, perhaps never finding it. Then comes hopeless

resignation, lassitude, loss of drive. Things once thought essential to living become unimportant.

The pain of loneliness produces much the same effect. It destroys the quality of life. It robs us of youth and can rob us of life itself. It drains us of our drive, takes away our concern for personal appearance and even destroys our interest in personal hygiene. Of course I'm talking about the effects of a profound loneliness such as might come with the death of a child, desertion by one's mate, or a sense of abandonment by society.

Aloneness Makes Us Vulnerable

I sometimes look at the plains that stretch out in every direction from my home, and I try to imagine what they were like five hundred years ago. In 1484 they were utterly uninhabited. Even the American Indian did not choose to live here at that early date. In my imagination I try to erase from this prairie the marks left by humans: roads, power lines, windmills, houses, trees, grain elevators, fences, cultivated fields. The mental picture left when I've finished erasing is of a sky unbroken by vapor trails, marked only by high-flying, wispy mare's tails. Also left is an uninterrupted vastness of prairie stretching to the horizon in every direction. Grass waves high in the wind that sweeps down from the mountains far to the west.

At times I imagine a buffalo herd moving slowly southward as it grazes. I hear the lowing of the cows calling their calves to nurse and the bellow of the bulls as one shakes his great shoulders and rolls over to wallow in the dust where he has staked claim to his harem.

As the herd moves on, I can see an old bull left behind, no longer able to keep up. He grazes alone for many days, and the air becomes colder. One morning he wakens to find his coat filled with snow and the prairie grasses bowing low under its weight. The winds climb and the snow comes horizontally, borne with great force upon the gale. This bothers the old bull not at all. He is made in such a way that he overcomes such weather with great ease.

But in the gray light of another morning he lifts his great head, shakes the snow from it and sees a single form silhouetted on a rise of ground a short distance away. He can see the newcomer's breath cloud in the cold predawn air. The bull feels a restlessness, a drive to move. And then voices come to his ears, high, sometimes in long, lingering calls, sometimes in staccato yips. Many forms join the one whose shadow stands on the hill. The pack lingers, milling for an uncertain moment, and then they plunge down, encircling the old one. Their gray, snow-flecked coats bristle in the cold, and their lips draw back from murderous white teeth.

The old giant stands his ground. His hooves flail out and his black horns toss one after another of the marauders broken and bloody into the snow. But there are too many for only one to fight. Even had he been younger it would have been an impossible battle. A flank is ripped on one side, and as he turns to defend the flank, another wolf catches his lip and jaw on the other side. At last he is pulled down to die, just as many thousands of his ancestors died before him. His fate became certain on the very day he left the herd to live alone.

Coming back from my world of thought, I remember that even as a man of the twentieth century, I am not so far removed from the way of the old bull's death. Some practices in the Eskimo culture are much like that. When an Eskimo grows old and feels of no more use to his people, he separates from the family so as not to burden them and wanders out onto the tundra or to an ice field, sits down and waits to be killed and eaten by a polar bear. He believes that later, when the bear itself is killed and eaten, his flesh will nourish the grandchildren he once loved.[1]

When one stops to think about it, one realizes that the veneer of civilization is very thin. I remember a time when I was eighteen years old, six hundred miles from home and living alone in a house in the country. Very early one morning I awoke to a vague feeling of nausea. In a short while the nausea had grown strong and I was miserably sick. I don't recall how long the sickness lasted or where it came from. What I do remember is the pain and the realization: "So this is what it's like to be sick with no one to help me!" Such a possibility had never occurred to me before. In every childhood fever and illness I had felt my mother's cool hand on my forehead and had been comforted by her tender care. Now I saw that sickness and aloneness make a terrible combination. Such helplessness. The total absence of loving sympathy. The danger if the sickness is lethal.

My point is that we are extremely vulnerable when we are alone. If man needed other human beings before the Fall when all was well and no threat of harm existed, then surely that need has been amplified many times over. When people became prey to wild beasts, to other people and to illness and injury, it became a matter of life and death to be part of a protecting group. Two or more could build protection against the elements better than one. Incapacitated for whatever reason, one without another to help would perish as surely as the weakened buffalo left to face the wolf pack alone.

It is said by some psychologists that infants have only two or three built-in fears, and that one of them is the fear of abandonment. Imagine, if you are still young, how you will feel as you grow old and your strength gradually fades. It is not only mobility that you will lose, but also some of the basic skills required for taking care of yourself. In every stage of life we need others.

Throughout history, there have been only a few short periods when it has been safe for a child or woman to walk alone in the cities or countrysides. It is certainly unsafe to-day. Companionship is a normal need, even for physical survival.

If there is any truth in the idea that the collective experiences of humanity in some way leave a mark on one's genetic code, it is no wonder that we respond with such dread to being alone.

When we become lonely, a restlessness sets in. The "empty feeling" that is so common demands to be filled. It becomes almost impossible to rest, to concentrate, to become involved in a good book or the plot of a television story. Always there is the drive to go out, to be among people, to hear their voices even though the words are not directed to us. Is this restlessness part of a built-in response to being lonely? Is it a driving search for the person or persons who will help us to survive? Perhaps.

Loneliness Causes Temptation
Beyond the threat it poses to bodily life, loneliness also threatens our spiritual well-being. It creates at least three kinds of temptation. First, there is the temptation to withdraw into oneself because of the pain that comes from loneliness. Rather than going out and cultivating friendships that would fill the emptiness, one may go deeper and deeper into isolation. The hermit and the catatonic are examples of this. But of course most of us will never go quite so far as these.

Along with this withdrawal may come a depression. A depressed person must put forth a herculean effort to overcome the inertia of depression and to work at even small tasks. The lonely housewife may not feel like doing the normal work of the home. She may neglect the children, forget housekeeping, sleep away her days or even try to escape through alcohol. The lonely employee may lose interest in her work. A high schooler may have no drive left to

pursue his studies; he may withdraw and fail to develop a
social life. The cycle deepens. Rather than gaining new support and friendships, the depressed person places a strain
on the ones he or she now has. The temptation to withdraw
is a serious one indeed.

A second temptation is toward a distorted view of life.
Personal values fade and one may feel, "I'm no good. If I
were, I would have friends. I'm truly a worthless person."

This is a normal response to abandonment. For example,
I know an eight-year-old boy named Joey whose father left
home and moved to a community six hundred miles away.
Joey believed that his father did not love him enough to
stay at home, and Joey took this as a personal pronounce-
ment of his unworthiness.

A year and a half later, Joey's mother decided it would be
best for Joey if they moved to the town where his father
had gone. But tragically, shortly after Joey and his mom
moved, his father's new girlfriend was transferred to a
distant state, and the father followed her. Later when Joey
came to our home, he sat at our table and said, "I wanted so
badly to be near my dad. And now that we've moved here,
he just up and leaves me again. He must not love me very
much." What sensitive person could hear such a thing and
not feel like weeping? Loneliness? Certainly! Destructive to
his sense of self-value? Beyond doubt!

Another way loneliness distorts one's view of reality has
to do with God. "If God exists, would he let me be hurt so
badly?" Or, "Only a very bad God would have permitted
my husband to die." Loneliness may tempt us to conclude
that God is bad or that he does not exist at all.

Loneliness tempts us to withdraw from others, to lose
our sense of self-worth and to doubt the existence or character of God. Loneliness also tempts us to enter into *wrong*
relationships. The pain of loneliness goes away when a
young girl finds an exciting new group and becomes a

part of it. And when a man enters into a relationship with a woman who powerfully attracts him, the excitement, the dreams of the future and the sexual involvement drive out the leaden weight that has caused pain. So far as the pain is concerned, it doesn't matter whether the young girl's group is a youth fellowship or promiscuous sorority. For the man, immediate relief comes from the new involvement whether it takes place in the context of legitimate courtship and marriage or in the context of an illicit affair.

The popularity of country and western music in the United States amazes me. In the last fifteen years, it has moved over the land like a great wave. Why? There may be a number of reasons, but surely the words of the songs have something to do with it.

The words don't talk much about the old West anymore, "Tumbling Tumbleweeds," "Give me land, lots of land," or things of that kind. They tell about deficits in relation-ships: loneliness, broken marriage, infidelity, desertion, fighting. Think of some of the songs from the last decade or so: "Daddy, Don't You Walk So Fast," "Jolene," "Make the World Go Away," and so on. Sometimes these songs are a direct plea for companionship, and often illegitimate com-panionship. In "Help Me Make It through the Night," we hear a plea for a woman to ignore what's right or wrong, to "let the devil take tomorrow," and to be a friend to a man who faces a lonely night.

Some marriages break up and some infidelities occur be-cause of sexual attraction alone or out of predatory motive —men or women looking for new sexual excitement. But it appears to me that even strong sexual attraction is not enough to cause people to violate their moral values to the extent we see it happening today. Consequently, I wonder how many illicit sexual relationships begin, not out of sex-ual attraction, but out of loneliness. How many people, feel-ing abandoned by their mates, meet someone who shows interest in them as a person and suddenly feel, "I've found a friend!" There must be many thousands who have not gone looking, who are not sexual predators, but who have become fornicators and adulterers out of great loneliness.

In a research article in *Psychology Today*, Maggie Scarf discusses women who have become sexually promiscuous. She notes that much promiscuity among women is preceded by periods of feeling abandoned, unloved. She also notes that the behavior is "a frantic effort to ward off feelings of isolation, abandonment, and depression, a kind of anti-depressant maneuvering."[2]

Scarf points out that, for the women she studied, promiscuity was to no avail. In spite of the fact that in the excitement of these escapades loneliness and its pain was forgotten, promiscuous behavior produced no security, no intimacy, nor any safe shelter "within the harbor of a trusting and satisfying relational bond."[3] The very object of the affair was not attained. Loneliness has such power. Even those who care a great deal about right and wrong may close their eyes to moral considerations. In the words of the song, "I don't care what's right or wrong. I don't try to understand." The immediate desire is for companionship; tomorrow is not part of the equation. "Let the devil take tomorrow. Tonight I need a friend."

None of these things in any way justifies bad behavior. I point them out so we can see that loneliness is not just some innocuous little flirtation with self-pity, nor is it just a painful condition to be endured stoically. Rather it is a dangerous road that winds through deep woods. From it run many side paths that dead-end in fatal traps. When we are gripped with loneliness, it is well worth our time and effort by the grace of God to fight our way out of it. We are much like the old buffalo. We become vulnerable to attack when we are outside of life's intended relationships. Little wonder then that God has pronounced loneliness "not good."

Part Two

Meeting Our Needs for Companionship

3

God

"Thou hast made us for Thyself,
and the heart of man is restless until
it finds its rest in Thee."
***Saint Augustine,* Confessions**

ON OCTOBER 30, 1938, WRITER, actor and director Orson Welles brought panic to thousands in the United States with his broadcast of H. G. Wells's *The War of the Worlds.* You may recall what took place.

Welles was in charge of CBS's weekly "Mercury Theater on the Air" and had chosen the classic story of a Martian invasion of Earth for that week's presentation. He and his codirectors had decided that the dramatization stood its best chance of success if presented as an eyewitness news report, and they had written the script accordingly. Martian landing was to occur at Grovers Mills, New Jersey. State police were said to be rushing to the site. A reporter gave a moment-by-moment account of the emergence of the foul, leathery heads of Martian invaders. The reporter's style was modeled after Herbert Morrison's actual newscast of the explosion of the Hindenburg at Lakehurst, New Jersey, two years before.

It was an intensely emotional account, with the reporter vomiting at the revolting sight just as Morrison had when he saw the burning bodies falling from the Hindenburg. Every effort was made to make the dramatization sound like a real event. The portrayal included the death of the reporter by Martian ray, a battle with the army in the Wachung Hills, the advance of the invaders across the Hudson and much more.

Of course at the program's beginning appropriate announcements had been made. But on that Sunday evening most radio listeners had been tuned to the Charlie McCarthy—Edgar Bergen program across the dial. In an interlude between Bergen's acts, many thousands twisted the dial, landed in the middle of Orson Welles's "newscast," and took it to be the real thing.

Police switchboards were flooded. Families rushed from their houses with wet towels over their faces. Some volunteered to fight, and one woman called the *Boston Globe* to say that she could see the glow of the fires in the distance. Students in dormitories lined up at the telephones to talk to their parents one last time. At least one woman tried to commit suicide, and many rushed to churches to pray. The Kansas City Bureau of the Associated Press received calls from coast to coast. The panic was not universal, but it was substantial!

At the broadcast's halfway point the announcer came on, his voice suave and bright: "You are listening to the CBS presentation of Orson Welles and the Mercury Theater on the Air in an original dramatization of *The War of the Worlds*, by H. G. Wells. The performance will continue after a brief intermission."[1] The phones in the studio began to ring and blue-uniformed police converged on the CBS building. Welles and his cast were horror-struck at what they had done. In the days that followed there was talk of legal action, but the casualties were not so many nor so severe as had first been believed, and all litigation was dropped.

Forty years later, an American space probe landed on Mars and began to test the soil and atmosphere for signs of life. At last American scientists made their report: "There is no sign of life on the planet Mars." I suppose it was because Orson Welles had been the controlling genius in the "Martian invasion of 1938" that the news media asked for his response to the scientists' conclusion. He reportedly answered, "I feel so alone!"

Did Welles intend his answer to be humorous? Or did he really feel a deep sadness, a sense of loss at the discovery that life does not exist on Mars? I can't say, but perhaps even at a cosmic level we want to be assured that the human race does not exist in isolation. It is not enough to live in a house with a family, in a town with friends, in a nation with two hundred twenty million compatriots. It is not even enough to live in a world with hundreds of countries and tribes. We want and need something more—the presence of Someone beyond humanity. If every planet in the universe were populated and every creature a personal friend of mine, still I would have an empty place within. For there is a space in my heart that can be filled only by a Friend who knows all my quirks and eccentricities, my deepest dreams and fears, my failures and successes. I want and need the friendship of Someone who unites me to my fellow men and women, both in a mystical and in an earthly way. I want to be the friend of One who gives my life purpose beyond the immediate day, who gives me value beyond what I do and what I seem to be. I need a relationship that transcends this world and all worlds. I crave talking with the One who created it all and having him actually call me his friend. I want to enjoy him and to have him enjoy me!

Why I Believe He Is There
I know that some people would read those last statements

and say, "Yes. Those cravings made man invent God." But I respond, "That's your guess. I say that man has these cravings because God made man for himself. The atheist calls the cravings cause, I call them effect." I don't contend for a moment that all, or even most, know that they long for God. Some seem to sense no incompleteness at all without him. But humanity has an empty place that is large, and we seem continually stretching to fill it. Yet neither things, nor human persons, nor events, nor earthly purpose can take his place.

The thought climate of the past one hundred or so years has left a great many not knowing whether this God whom we crave exists at all. It is as though some men and women of science and philosophy have sent out a space probe, analyzed the data and reported to the world, "There is no evidence that God exists anywhere." And the race has responded, "I feel so alone!" But Christians stand and call to a waiting, empty world, in the words of Francis Schaeffer, "He *is* there, and he is not silent!"[2]

I want to share with you an experience that gave me great confidence that God is there. I first believed in Christ at the age of eight. Afterward I had no serious doubts about God's existence until about the age of twenty-seven. At that time I was enrolled in graduate school, studying psychology. The head of the department was an atheist who believed that man is a machine, nothing more, and that spiritual experiences are simply autosuggestion. I was shaken by his arguments, and I feared that life was about to make a sudden, drastic change for me. I prayed, "Lord, if you are really there, help me to know. Give me reasons that can't be called autosuggestion."

In the weeks that followed, some thoughts came into my mind. I had never thought of them before. I did not read them somewhere or hear them from someone. I concluded that they were the answer to my prayer, and they gave me a more solid foundation for believing that God really is.

First, I saw that the existence of an infinite person is not contradictory to reason. After all, on a physical level we admit the infinity of space. If mathematics lays claim to understanding the infinity of space, may there not be a higher law allowing the infinity of personality? Can one really talk about God's being subject to any law, known or unknown? I saw that it was not ridiculous to believe in God.

Second, the fact that mankind is a conscious and self-aware being struck me with great force. Consciousness is as stunning a fact as existence itself! The atheist explains it as the result of the complex chemical, electrical functions of the brain. But has any scientist ever produced self-awareness in the laboratory? Could any researcher show that the synthesis of any elements could produce consciousness? No. Therefore the conclusion that an amalgam of elements could bring forth a conscious person, rather than being demonstrable scientific fact, is just as great an act of faith as the Christian conclusion that God is the origin of consciousness.

Isn't human self-awareness a testimony to the existence of something beyond mechanics? Something called "spirit" or "life"? I decided that it is. Does life or spirit testify to the existence of an intelligent Creator? I decided that it does.

Next, while it was not a new thought to me, the orderly nature of the universe impressed itself upon me. Voltaire said, "The world embarrasses me, and I cannot think that this watch exists and has no watchmaker."[3] Voltaire's embarrassment was my strength and comfort. It was not only not *illogical* to believe in the existence of an infinite person, there was good reason to believe! The possibility became the necessity. But who was he? What was his name?

Then I thought of the Bible, its unity, its moral plane, its message. Its internal qualities were evidence that it was not merely the contrivance of human thought, and that it could be trusted as a message from beyond human reach.

And then there was the resurrection of Christ, giving testimony that what he spoke was true and that he had come from the Father. So now this infinite person had a name, "I Am," and again I had a way to him through Jesus Christ. Now the beauty of the relationship returned and my assurances went deeper than ever before. It was now clear that my fellowship with him had not been "one talker aping two."[4] It had not been autosuggestion. He really was there.

But Did He Love Me?

Though we may be persuaded that God is there, we may not be convinced that he wants contact with humanity. After all, why should he be interested in me?

I once believed that God was lonely and that he created us to meet that need. As James Weldon Johnson said in his poem "Creation,"

And God stepped out on space,
And He looked around and said:
"I'm lonely—
I'll make me a world."[5]

Of course if one believes this, one can also easily believe that God wants human company. But I began to think, "That can't be true! After all, there has always been perfect fellowship in the Trinity. God is perfectly sufficient in himself." However, after thinking along those lines for a while, I began to see that after all God may have chosen to create within himself a desire for this hairless little biped, and therefore a need.[6] And if a need, then a possibility for loneliness—God making himself vulnerable to pain! I don't know just what theologians might think about that idea, but it is very satisfying to me, and I have not yet found scriptural grounds for denying it.

In coming to believe that God chooses to be lonely for us, I had restored all the wonder and affection of the tender

God who created us, in my view not because he needed us, but more—because he *wanted* to need us. And it may be that I can go one step further and say that my very capacity for loneliness, whether for God or for my fellow human beings, may be a copy of God's capacity to be lonely. Might this not be another part of what it means to be created in his image?

Reconciliation

To be persuaded that God exists is important. It's just as important to know that he wants fellowship with me. But the desire is not the fulfillment. There are substantial walls that continue to separate me from him.

First of all, God is the moral ruler of the universe, and the human race has rebelled against his moral order. We are outlaws, and a great gulf is fixed between God and us. Though I believe that God exists, my problem of loneliness for him is not solved unless (1) I can come back from rebellion into his good graces and (2) I can actually have an ongoing friendship with him following the reconciliation.

Think of what it means to be reconciled with God. On God's part it means his continual love in spite of our rebellion. Out of his love he sent Christ to die in our place, taking our punishment. In Christ we are assured that the gulf between us is gone; that is, we can be assured of it as we receive him according to the terms of John 1:12. This passage promises us not only reconciliation, but sonship and daughtership as well. Paul spoke of this reconciliation in his letter to the gentile Ephesians:

> Remember that you were . . . separated from Christ, alienated . . . strangers . . . having no hope and without God in the world. But now in Christ Jesus you who once were far off have been brought near in the blood of Christ. For he is our peace, . . . that he might . . . reconcile us . . . to God, . . . thereby bringing the hostility to an end. (Eph 2:12-16)

On our part reconciliation to God means laying down our weapons and surrendering to him. It means believing in Christ, trusting God to forgive through his blood. It means confession of his lordship with our own lips. (See Romans 10:8-10.)

It is profoundly satisfying to know that God and I are no longer at odds. This is peace in its most important sense. It is the beginning of the most vital of all friendships.

Developing the Friendship
In human relationships a mere introduction to another person does not mean that a wonderful friendship is ahead. Even reconciliation after long separation may only mean that barriers have been removed. If true warmth and companionship are to exist, there is much work to be done.

In the same way, a great many have Christ as Savior but never know much of him as Friend, except perhaps in the sense that he is there to be called upon when they need him. But I am not suggesting that we try to make God our "buddy." He is not that, cannot be that because of who he is and what we are. We may respect a buddy but we hardly revere him or her. At the same moment we must remember that the relationship with God can become very real and full, with all the elements of true companionship. We can be fully open with him, complain to him, express our doubts, our joys. We can feel the warmth of the feathers of his wings (Ps 91:4), see his power exercised in our behalf, sense his great personal love (Jn 3:16), and in many ways know his actual presence.

We can think of those in Scripture who were spoken of as God's friends. Abraham is called God's friend in Isaiah 41: 8 and James 2:23. David was said to be a "man after his own heart" (1 Sam 13:14 and Act 13:22). Moses reached a great height of friendship with God. We read about him, "Thus the LORD used to speak to Moses face to face, as a man speaks to his friend" (Ex 33:11). Fulfilling the deepest human desires, Jesus said to his disciples, "I have called you friends" (Jn 15:15). These words open up the floodgates of the deepest and highest personal satisfaction possible.

But how can I develop that kind of relationship with God? Assuming that I have made Jesus my Savior and Lord, how can I also make him my Friend?

Drawing Closer to God

In seventeenth-century France, a big, awkward man who had been a footman and a soldier wanted to know the Lord in the intimate way we have been talking about here. Nicholas Herman was converted to Christ at the age of eighteen. In 1666, at the age of sixty-one, he entered the Carmelite Order in Paris as a lay brother and assumed the name Brother Lawrence. However, joining the order did not give him leisure for full-time prayer and Bible study. In fact he was given kitchen work, something he very much disliked. But this was no hindrance to his pursuit of God. He continued to work in the kitchen almost until his death at the age of eighty. In that time he attained a sense of God's presence that most of us never come to know.

After his death some of his conversations and letters were published under the title *The Practice of the Presence of God.*[7] Nearly three hundred years have passed, and earnest Christians everywhere still read his book, trying to learn the lessons he learned in that monastery kitchen. Using Brother Lawrence's life as an illustration, we can find at least three important principles for developing our own relationship with God.

First, there is *the principle of obedience.* Brother Lawrence said, "I would not take up a straw from the ground against his order."[8] He was concerned that he would offend God by sinning, and when he felt that he had offended him, he immediately repented. One cannot read his book thoughtfully and fail to see that this man believed God's friendship to depend in part on his own personal obedience.

Is this scriptural? Is obedience related to fellowship? There are those, perhaps a good many, who feel perfect freedom to call on God at any time, professing great intimacy with him, but who seem to give no thought to obeying him. But in John 14:21 Jesus says, "He who has my commandments and keeps them, he it is who loves me; and he who loves me will be loved by my Father, and I will love him and manifest myself to him." This verse promises three things: the Father's love, the Son's love, and in some undefined way, a very personal self-revelation of Jesus. But these promises are only for those who love him and demonstrate their love by obeying him.

At first one might think God is saying we must merit his love. In one sense he does not say that at all, and in another that is exactly what he says. Let me explain by putting it like this: (1) God loves all people; (2) God has a special kind of love for those who have become his sons and daughters in Christ; (3) he has a deeper friendship-love for those who love him to the degree that they seek strongly to obey him. When in response to our obedient love Jesus says that he will manifest himself to us, I believe he means that he will cause us to experience himself as a very real person, our warm, dear Friend.

Next is *the principle of reaching out.* Brother Lawrence actively sought God. He had an inner drive much like the psalmist's, "As a hart longs for flowing streams, so longs my soul for thee, O God" (Ps 42:1). This drive caused him to pray and study the Scriptures. In his earlier days he spent many hours in devotional pursuits, and he advised others, "He is always near you and with you; leave Him not alone."[9] This is James 4:8 in action: "Draw near to God and he will draw near to you."

God makes overtures to us and waits patiently for our

response. But relationships of depth develop only when we take initiatives of our own, exercising the principle of reaching out to God.

Last is *the principle of seeing the unseen.* The faith chapter, Hebrews 11, has much to say about this. Verse one says that faith is the "conviction of things not seen," and verse three, that the world was created "out of things which do not appear." Enoch was able to please God and to walk with him because he believed.

Brother Lawrence spoke of walking in God's presence. He cultivated the habit of thinking of God as always by his side and of talking with him about the matters of life as they came up. He called this "practicing the presence of God." He was "seeing the unseen."

We often use the word *imagine* to mean producing a mental image of something that isn't real. But the word means more than that. We can also produce mental images of things that *are* real but can't be seen. After all, there are a great many real things that can be seen only in the mind. For example, the conventional diagram of the atom came from a mentally created image, but an atom is quite real. Depression is "blue," anger is "red," envy is "green." We use such visualizations every day.

Friendship with God is real, yet we have never seen God sitting and talking with anyone. We are left to our own ability to create a mental picture of this reality, a reality that we perceive through faith. If we use our ability to create this image in a habitual way as Brother Lawrence did, we experience a new dimension in our walk with the Lord. Augustine said, "God is more truly imagined than expressed, and he exists more truly than is imagined."[10]

Brother Lawrence was different from many great devotional writers in that he did not emphasize isolation from others in order to be in God's presence. He did have times of private prayer, but not to the extent that many others did. He emphasized being in conversation with God at all times, no matter how many others were about. He himself was very much in the company of others. One of the benefits of his approach to prayer is that with it the noise of twentieth-century living cannot deprive us of God. He said, "The time of business does not with me differ from the time of prayer, and in the noise and clatter of my kitchen, while several persons are at the same time calling for different things, I possess God in as great tranquility as if I were upon my knees at the blessed sacrament."[11]

I admire this man, for I am afraid that many of us make prayer all too much a time of obligation, filling it with recitals of our failures, fears, wants and efforts to attain some mysterious state of holiness. We confuse repentance with self-flagellation and spend much of our prayer time beating ourselves down. This pairs God with pain, and we condition ourselves to see our times with him as a world of unpleasantness. On the contrary, Brother Lawrence was in God's presence no matter what emotion he was experiencing. God became his constant friend and companion, not just his confessor.

His Friendship Makes Us Full

When we are reconciled to God and walking with him as our Friend, everything changes. All objects we possess, all persons we call our own, everything has a different meaning. Because I know him even the stars look different. In spite of their great distance they seem friendly and even related to me since the same hand made us both. The glow of the sun's disk on the horizon radiates a warmth that is more than physical fire. The dew glistening in the flower's deep blue heart has an overwhelming beauty that is more than light and color. The face of both stranger and friend take on new meaning because we are related in a new way. Again I say, it is profoundly satisfying to know that God and I are no longer at odds! The universe literally sings with me!

Some time ago the editors of *Psychology Today* surveyed their readers on the subject of friendship.[12] Forty thousand readers responded. The surveyors asked what qualities the respondents valued most in a friendship. Their answers showed that these led the field: loyalty, warmth, affection, supportiveness and willingness to "make time for me." Loyalty was defined as "staying with me when I am down, keeping my secrets, accepting me, staying with me even when I am wrong, supporting me in trouble, understanding me." On reflection, we realize that these are the very qualities God brings into a relationship. Others may desert us, and we may even feel that God has forsaken us. Yet he has not. We can never be fully alone again. The writer of the letter to the Hebrews encouraged his readers by saying, "He has said, 'I will never fail you nor forsake you' " (Heb 13:5). David had said centuries before, "My father and my mother have forsaken me, but the LORD will take me up" (Ps 27:10).

For my own part, I often think of God and me as friends. I do not imply that we are equal. He is God, and I am his creature. Even so in the best of times I am able to think of our friendship without any thought of what he can do for me or what I can do for him. In those times we become simply two good friends enjoying each other. There is closeness, rest, a security that I cannot express in any way. It is as though the two of us were intended from all eternity to belong to each other. It is as though the galaxy and everything in it belongs to us, and yet no part of it intrudes on our being together. While he is not always the *focal point* of my thoughts, he is always present in my mind, always there "in the corner of my eye." It is almost as if, should I turn my head quickly enough, I could see him. I am deeply grateful that through Christ he has made himself available to fill the God-shaped vacuum in my heart.

Our loneliness for God, then, is a loneliness that can always be healed. It is not always easy to find good human friends. Mobility and our highly technical society militate against community, family and permanent friendships. But God has made himself available to each of us through Jesus Christ.

One of the added benefits of having found him as Friend is this: we are in a much better position to go out and find human friends to fill the other empty places in our lives.

4

Family

"The family was ordained of God . . .
the first form of the church on earth."
Pope Leo XIII

"CHARLES, DID YOU HEAR THAT?" It was Dad's quiet voice waking me from a sound sleep. The house was dark at four in the morning, and no one else was stirring. The bed was warm and comfortable. I sat up to listen.

Our little house was set near a narrow gravel road in an oak woods in the Red River Valley of north Texas. It was winter, 1947, and I was eight years old. "There it is again!" From somewhere in the woods came a sound like the falling of a giant crystal chandelier, a crash accented by a clear, high, tinkling sound. I had no idea what could make such a strange noise, and in the hush that followed I asked, "Daddy, what is it?"

Sitting beside me on the bed in the dark, warm house, Dad told me that in the night a slow, gentle rain had fallen, and that as it fell it froze to everything it touched—the roof, the walls, the well rope, the electric lines and, of course, the trees. Even small twigs, he said, were coated with an inch or more of ice. Young trees stood with their tops bowed to the ground. What I had heard was the ice coating falling off an oak.

Hours later the sun's first rays spilled over the horizon into the woods, and the world came alive with color. Literally millions of crystalline prisms broke the sun's morning light into all the colors of the rainbow. Brilliantly pure white light flashed through the clear, cold morning air.

Dad broke the ice from the well bucket and from the coiled rope so he could draw the morning's supply of water. My younger brother, sister and I slipped, frolicked and slid over the icy ground to our hearts' content.

Everywhere electric lines were down. The old Oldsmobile's radio brought us the message, "No school today," and as good or better, the factory in town was closed because of the downed power lines. Dad would be home! Unbounded joy! Just the five of us, Dad, Mom, and the three children, with a day (three days as it turned out) to enjoy as a family, uninterrupted in play and work by any outside annoyance.

Family Far Away
Now I'm forty-five, and I treasure that memory of early days at home. But in the intervening years the outside world has intruded, forced us apart, placing many miles between us. When the family was complete there were seven of us. Now Mom and Dad are in their seventies and still live within ten miles of that little house. I live nearly six hundred miles away, while my brothers and sisters live one hundred eighty, two hundred fifty, and a thousand miles away. Only one brother remains nearby.

Our family is not unusual. These days it is perfectly normal for children to scatter to the four winds. When I return to the town of thirty thousand people where I attended high school, I walk along the downtown streets and through the mammoth new shopping mall and search in vain for a face I know from my high-school days. I look through the telephone directory to find names of old friends, but they are not there. Like me, they have moved away.

Every year forty million Americans, one in every five, move. This new pattern has an immense power to shape the lives of the nation's people. Most importantly, it divides the family.

When the family is not present to do its normal work, one result is loneliness. Gradually we are learning that we are really not equipped to survive well without this basic support group.

Loneliness can even bring death. James J. Lynch is a specialist in psychosomatic medicine at the University of Maryland Medical School and author of *The Broken Heart: The Medical Consequences of Loneliness.* Dr. Lynch argues that isolation can bring on emotional and physical illness. He makes comparisons between societies that have strong family units and those that do not and concludes that death rates from heart disease are significantly higher among those who live in settings where families are not close. He places special emphasis on family and community life and then says, "Simply put, there is a biological basis for our need to form human relationships. If we fail to fulfill that need, our health is in peril."[1]

What Does the Family Do for Us?

The family is God's plan for individual survival and development. The tenor of Scripture is profamily, and the experience of the race as a whole points to the family as the basic unit of survival.

At the most obvious level *the family provides for us physically.* In an optimum situation, a man and a woman bring us to birth on an island of stability. They give us food, shelter from the elements, protection from animals and from malicious humans. Without these basic things the human child could not survive for even a short time.

But the family also meets less obvious needs. *It provides for us emotionally.* During World Wars 1 and 2 many infants died in hospital nurseries. These children were given adequate food, warm beds, good shelter, and yet they wasted away. It was finally determined that their deterioration came from the lack of touching, being held and caressed, and other tokens of affection that good parents provide.[2] This need does not disappear as we grow older, for touch communicates the message of love, support and belonging.

An adult with a background of warm, accepting love is better prepared to venture out into the larger world, for he or she has a sense of strength and support that gives courage for facing life's tasks. In the same way that children explore and play only when they know that Mother is nearby, adults venture out confidently only if a stable family has given them a sense of unconditional security.

The family *shows us how to live.* It gives us our earliest impressions of what life should be like. The older members are models for us. We see what responses and actions are appropriate under given circumstances; we learn to work, how to care for ourselves and how to give order to our lives.

The family also *gives us our ideas about God.* Although this is not true in every case, most who have a relationship with God were led into it by their parents. The epigraph at the beginning of this chapter points to a deeper kind of survival skill imparted by the family—the spiritual dimension of survival. The first form of the church on earth was indeed the family, and it is still the most basic, most essential part of the church. It teaches the Scriptures, models the Christlike life and otherwise points its members toward God.

The Family Supports Us in Adulthood
Our need for family life does not end when we turn eight-

een. Leaving home to go away to school was an exciting time for me. With new friends, activities and surroundings I felt no homesickness at all the first year. But during the second year, strong yearnings for home began to surface, and they continue to this day. I was in the process of discovering my continuing need for family.

In his book *Loneliness: The Experience of Emotional and Social Isolation* Robert Weiss tells of Rose, a woman in her late thirties. Rose was divorced, had two children and hoped to marry a man named Harold. But Harold dropped her quite suddenly, and she was left an emotional shambles. However, Rose still lived in the town where she had grown up, and her family was nearby. Her mother, brother and sisters loved her and took an active role in seeing her through this crisis. They sympathized, came by often, wept with her, gave good advice that she accepted and even introduced her to the man she eventually married. Had Rose been alone in a distant city, one wonders just how she would have gotten along. It is likely that her family brought her through the crisis in a way that friends could not have done.[3]

With our need for family support from birth to death, it is not hard to see why we become lonely without the family. It fills a very basic biological, emotional, spiritual need.

The Family in Trouble

American families in great numbers are in trouble. It seems that almost every parent with adult children has one child who is divorced. The extended family is also being divided at a terrible rate, being dispersed across the length and breadth of the continent. The family's time-tested support systems are unavailable to many, and the emotional outcome in terms of loneliness is great.

What has caused these changes? The past one hundred years have altered American social structure in substantial ways. Some of these alterations have worked against the family rather than for it. For example, look at some of the forces that are working against the *extended* family.

We once were a rural nation. As the frontier moved on to the West and the settlements changed from pockets of chaos to orderly communities, family life became quite stable. Children were born in a community; they were raised there, found their life's work and their mates there and eventually died there. That may sound dull to a people accustomed to mobility, but it made for a strong extended family. One was surrounded by grandparents, parents, aunts, uncles, cousins, nieces, nephews and one's own off-spring. Together they acted as a support system that kept its members "on the straight and narrow."

World War 2 seems to be the dividing point. Since the midforties the extended family has disintegrated. It hardly occurred to most folk that a bad thing was happening. In a way it was just the grand fulfillment of the American dream for a wider, fuller, more exciting life. Given the ease of travel, it was not as though we would never see our families again. Besides, there is always the telephone, and we do have an obligation to ourselves and to our spouses and children to work our way up in the world. And often working our way up meant leaving the home community.

Probably the most powerful force pulling against the extended family has been economic. In the past, businesses were locally owned, and people not employed in business owned or worked on a farm. Today a great many businesses are owned and operated by chains with headquarters half a continent away. Those who work for such firms must sometimes choose between losing work or moving to an-other location. Or the choice may be between a substantial wage increase and staying on in the home community at the old wage.

Faced with these alternatives the nuclear family is often

torn away from the extended family and loses its support. Counsel, emotional strength, a sense of belonging, a sense of obligation to the larger family's reputation and cohesion —all are lost. Weiss says this is why the nuclear family separated from the extended family is "a family at risk."[4]

The nation's businesses face their own obstacles to survival, but it appears to me that their priorities need to change for the sake of something more important than economics. The family needs to be recognized and treated like what it really is, the most important element in our social structure.

Another way in which the family is in trouble has to do with child care. Once again economics has something to do with the problem. Two things have worked together to change family structure: the economic need for two paychecks for each family, and women's new vision for self-expression outside the home. I doubt that either of these will change soon. But the fact that many children come home to empty houses and lack quality parenting must change.

One bright spot in this picture is that some business leaders are experimenting with flexible working hours that allow one parent to be at home when the children leave for school and one to be present when they return. With both parents working, the rigid eight-to-five system simply doesn't allow for quality home leadership.

The second great force against the family is individualism. The Bible encourages individuality, and our nation is built around the concept of the right of self-determination. But by *individualism* I mean a wrong application of the right of self-determination. I mean that everyone wants to be independent of others, to do his or her own thing, to follow his or her own personal star, to be free to go where he or she wants to go, to do what he or she wants to do and to be wholly self-determining.

It is an overextension of the concept of liberty to want to act as an individual even when it is not in the best interest of others. Choices about our work, our social life, our place of residence, even what risks to take and how to spend our leisure time must always be made with the family's best interests in mind.

Urie Bronfenbrenner is highly regarded as an authority in child development. In an interview with *Psychology Today*, Bronfenbrenner commented on the free-spirited American style of individualism. He said, "This whole way of life is fine if you're young, sexy, and full of verve. But if you happen to be a child, or sick, or lonely, or old—and all of us are at some time—you need somebody else. If that sombody else is doing his own thing, he's not there."[5]

Louise Bernikow, writing in the *New York Times,* says, "We want independence *and* a faithful lover, we want the support of family but not its demands."[6] Here is a terrible contradiction in desire: we want to be free to act as we will, but at the same time we want others to be reliable and supportive of us. This means that we desire something from others that we are not willing to give them in return. This frame of mind works powerfully against the family.

What happens to the person who deserts the family for the sake of personal autonomy? The classic example is Jesus' story of the prodigal son. The son took his inheritance and left the family in order to express his individualism, though in those days what he did was not called by so sophisticated a name.

He went to a distant city and joined a group of people who were also busy with self-expression. They were his friends because they were all after the same thing, and it worked well for them to develop some sort of symbiotic relationship in which they could all get something from the other group members. No doubt they all enjoyed themselves a great deal, but since the group was built on self-

expression and individuality, no one brought anything substantial into it to give the other members true strength and
stability.

Times got tough. What the young man had to offer the
group was gone, and they had nothing to give him. When
he was totally deprived of self-respect and had only enough
food to keep himself alive, he woke up and returned to the
only group that had ever accepted him enough and had
resources enough to rally around and help him when he
was in difficulty—his own family.

Jesus told this story as a parable of the lost being found.
God is the father, and the prodigal is any of us who choose to
leave God out. Though the prime point is that God is waiting to welcome us home if we repent, the lesson about the
foolishness of excessive individualism is also there.

But in the case of modern society and the family, the
story has a strange new twist. In our case the son has gone
off to express his individualism, but so has the older brother.
So has the mother. So has the father. Everyone is busy going in his or her own direction. When any one member gets
in trouble and decides to return to the shelter, no one else
is home! The father is as independent as the son, the
mother as the father, and so on. I know that not every
family lives that way, but a great many do.

So what is the result? Left unprotected, each must find
shelter as best he can. There are many injuries along the
way, and many deaths.

What does this have to do with loneliness? Everything.
Remember, *loneliness is the feeling that signals a deficit in relationships*. It is God's gift to us, in order to tell us that something is missing and that we need to take some kind of action.

Can Something Be Done?
What can we do? Can these forces working against the

family be brought to heel? I think they can. Business empires can be dealt with and made to change: labor unions have demonstrated this dramatically. When people unite to bring change they can succeed. The question is, do we care enough about this issue to unite and influence the system for the good of the family? The application of biblical principles by Christians in the business world can have a great effect on whether business continues to revolve around what is economically good and socially acceptable or around what is good for the family.

Regarding individualism, at least three things can be done. First, we must deal with it in our own hearts. We must confess that we have gone too far and that in going too far we have sinned. Then we must go forward as members one of another, acting in the best interests of our brothers and sisters.

Second, armed with facts about what happens when family members choose to act against the unit's best interests, we can try to educate others to the dangers of excessive individualism.

Third, we can confront the entertainment media that does so much to create our expectations and goals for living. There is a chance that, presented with a compelling case and massive popular support, the movers behind that world will develop more responsible behavior, giving us pictures of family life that more closely conform to biblical norms.

We can also work at raising our own view of the family to the high level that it deserves. For instance, we can structure our time in ways that bring the family together. I admit this is hard to do. An entire week can pass without a single meal at which every family member is present. A parent, overzealous about work, may spend late hours at a job, while another is absorbed excessively by social functions or volunteerism. Teen life is filled with activity: band, cheerleading, debating, sports and studies. A family may have to consciously plan and work to bring themselves together, and each member may need to sacrifice to reach the goal.

The church can contribute to the family's cohesiveness, for it is a family-oriented body. Or at least it should be. The epigraph at the beginning of this chapter is quite accurate. "The family was ordained of God . . . the first form of the church on earth." The church has been in the forefront of the fight for family life, establishing mental health services, marriage improvement groups and workshops, counseling services for troubled families, and a Christian framework in which families can worship, study and play together.

On the other hand, the church is sometimes guilty of dividing families unnecessarily, a trend that should be resisted. Every congregation ought to do all that it can to build and enhance family life.

Many Partings
We have devoted several pages to the forces at work against today's family. Now let's turn our attention to another problem: how one can combat the personal loneliness that comes from losing one's family.

About twenty years ago I read an account of a girl who had no family at all. Margaret Sangster told her story in "A Memory Can't Be Bought."[7] The girl, Mary, had written to Sangster, asking her to compose a special poem just for her. In her letter she included her story and a dollar bill as payment.

Mary had been left on the steps of an orphanage when she was a baby. Because she "wasn't very pretty or very smart" nobody adopted her. So Mary grew up in the orphanage. From there she went to live in her own apartment, working in a factory six days a week during World War 2. On Sundays she walked in the city park, and one day she met a soldier who was stationed just across the river. They began to see each other often.

For the first time in her life Mary had someone who loved her. They began to make marriage plans, and for the first time she had a future. Telling her story she said, "All I wanted was him and his love. All I wanted was somebody to belong to me." Soon Mary and Ross were married, and after a short while he was shipped overseas.

One day at work Mary fainted. She was expecting a baby. She was ecstatic! Sitting down that very afternoon, she wrote Ross a letter telling him the good news. But in one of those ironic twists that can scarcely be believed, as she was writing a messenger came to her door with a telegram from the War Department. Ross had been killed in action. She said, "I was stunned. . . . My husband was dead. I'd never feel his lips on mine again, but I had one comfort. I wasn't back where I'd started." Ross had left her with something that would be hers forever.

Mary had a little girl. She kept working to provide for herself and the baby, so the little one was placed in a day-care center. The two had little time together, and the only things the baby owned were the blanket for her crib and a celluloid rattle. But on Sundays the baby was all hers.

One day word came to Mary at the factory that the baby was ill and that she should come immediately. But before she reached the nursery, the little girl died. So, as Margaret Sangster said, "Mary *was* right back where she started—a girl not very pretty, nor very smart, but a girl who had a great talent for loving and giving." In her letter Mary asked Sangster to write a poem that would keep the baby from fading from her memory. The poem was written and sent to her in care of General Delivery. Mary picked up the letter. Though she tried, Margaret Sangster was never able to trace her and never heard from her again.

Mary never knew her parents or any of her extended family. She lost her husband to war and her little girl to illness. Sometimes we lose family members through fatal accidents, and sometimes by divorce or desertion. Some give their children away because they are financially unable to support them. Some have children taken from them by the courts. Other families divide because they cannot get along with each other. Husbands and wives drift apart, teenagers rebel or are alienated by unreasonable parents. Brothers and sisters compete with each other.

But for all that, the most common way to lose one's family is simply in the normal course of life. Parents live out their years and die. Children grow up and leave home. Along with our mates, we age, and eventually one of us slips away, leaving the other to live out the rest of life in the best way possible.

Even if no dissension, distance or premature death intervenes, yet one by one we lose each other. Toward the close of J. R. R. Tolkien's *The Return of the King* is a chapter whose title is the sad commentary on every family circle: "Many Partings." As surely as two come together, someday they will say good-by. And for most, the loss of family is the greatest loss of all.

Knowing that loss will come to each of us, how do we deal with it when it comes? More properly, how do we deal with the emotions of loneliness? The question is a hard one, for each of us is different in temperament, in background and in the resources from which we can draw. It is one thing to be lonely and young and another to be lonely and old. It is one thing to lose one's mate and have five children living nearby, and another to lose a mate and have no children at all. The trials of being lonely and rich are different from the trials of being lonely and poor. Recovery from loneliness will be different for the divorced person who is twenty years old than it will be for one who is sixty. Dealing with loneliness will be more difficult for one with an innate bent toward depression than for one who is naturally buoyant and happy.

But despite the diversity of personalities and situations, some very basic things can be said about dealing with this kind of loneliness, some of which will apply to everyone.

In the days after my oldest boy left home, I was taken by surprise by some of the emotions that swept through me. Mark's high-school graduation exercises had been on Monday evening. Tuesday morning, car loaded until the rear sank dangerously low, he was eager to go. Like most boys his age he was ready to try his wings. His destination was Columbus, Ohio, eleven hundred fifty miles from the small rural parsonage where we had lived for the past four years.

When the moment came for him to climb behind the wheel and drive away, I put my arms around him and wept. When he pulled out of the drive and disappeared down the road I felt miserably empty and alone. But I had expected all of that. What surprised me in the days that followed was the sadness I felt when I drove past the high school, for example. The building had seemed warm and friendly to me before, but now it was empty and unpleasant. Every evening I had felt good inside when I heard from my study the sound of his tires safely in our gravel drive. Though he was gone, I found myself listening for that sound. Then I would remember that I would not hear his tires in the drive in the same way ever again, and the emptiness would flood in upon me.

I slowly began to realize that I was grieving. It was not as though he were dead, but I grieved for his presence, for sunny, pleasant days together, for an era of his life and mine that was gone forever. The grieving was involuntary, and it was eased only by the thought that someday we might share life and nearness again, though I knew it would never be exactly the same.

The pain became less after a time. But as I write this, over a year and a half later, the emotions that had subsided rise to the surface again. He is still away. I still miss him more than I can say. The children left at home bring me much joy, yet nothing fills the empty place he left.

But I am no longer grieving. In this case, my recovery depended on several things. First, it depended on the confidence that God really does care for both of us and that no matter what happens, someday we will be together again in heaven, a place where there will be no more partings.

The second aid to recovery was the presence of my other children. Within a few days it dawned on me that it would be totally unfair to them for me to continue to grieve for Mark. I had to be willing to accept his absence and to invest my emotional energies in enjoying their presence. The third thing that helped was increased involvement in a hobby—re-enacting historical events—I had wanted to pursue for years. This brought me into contact with new friends and in some measure compensated for the loss. Perhaps it would be more accurate to say that it helped take my mind off my loss.

In dealing with the absence of family for any reason, try to keep in mind three things that we noted in chapter one. Number one, loneliness is our response to the lack of a relationship that we need. So the first step is to identify the deficit. We must ask, "What relationship is missing from my life?" This may be an easy question to answer. If you are without any family at all, you understand why you are lonely. If your mother or your husband has just passed away, the source of your feelings is apparent.

Second, to end loneliness one must develop relationships. There is something to be said for keeping busy with one's social life or throwing oneself into one's work. Staying busy and having good friends will help ease the pain. Allowing the ordeal to deepen one's relationship with God is certainly in order. But we also need to deepen and expand our human relationships, and we may have to work at doing it. Dr. Robert Weiss says, "I can offer no method for ending loneliness other than the formation of new relationships that might repair the deficit responsible for the loneliness."[8]

The third thing to remember is that one kind of relationship cannot fill the need for another kind. God gave us families for one set of reasons and community life for another. God placed a family-shaped vacuum in the human heart and only the family can fill it.

But if one has lost family, or if family is far away, how can it be replaced? In one sense it cannot. Yet things can be done to take up the slack.

Most of us expect to meet the need for family by leaving home and establishing a family of our own. College years are often only a brief interlude between the old family and the new. Yet there are a great many people who, for one reason or another, never find a mate. But I have observed many single people who deal with the absence of family very effectively. Whether they are away at college, living across the continent or separated from their family by death, a significant number deal with the deficit by adopting a family. In a family totally unrelated to them by blood, they have cultivated friendships, given and received warmth and love, and over a period of time become as much a son or daughter, sister or brother, father or mother, as any blood-related member of the group. That's a wonderful thing! The human heart is an open and receiving, giving, sharing entity that enjoys loving and being loved.

I believe that if I were to lose all my family ties I would seek a substitute family to fill those needs. But how are such contacts made? Those I have known have made them in the normal channels of life. A boy who had been put out of his home went to work for a farmer and his wife and became a permanent family member. A twenty-year-old fellow without parents or spouse moved to a large city to work in the aircraft industry. He rented a room in a home, and the family took him in as their own son. A teen-aged girl was thrown out of her home by an angry and unreasonable father. Wandering about, she was taken under the jurisdiction of the juvenile court and placed in foster care. Her foster parents loved her and eventually adopted her.

Single adults can reach out to families around them, "adopting" them and their children and being "adopted" in return. Single people and childless couples have become "aunts" and "uncles" to their friends' children, being included as family members on holidays and birthdays and sharing some of the burden of child care. Some single people live with a family they enjoy, while others open their own homes to friends and acquaintances, creating a warm and mutually supportive living situation. One woman I know has built a large extended family which includes former and present housemates, friends' children, married friends and international students. Every holiday season and almost every month brings a succession of friends to her door to renew close and ongoing relationships. Her extended family spreads all across the globe.

Yet there are times when efforts to establish such relationships with others do not work. Why? In order for the bonding to be sound, one has to be the right kind of person and find the right kind of family. By "right kind," I mean mutually compatible, with something substantial to offer to the relationship. In chapter ten I will discuss the basic elements of building friendships, and of course that will apply to building relationships with families as well.

The family is a necessary provision. It exists in different forms in different societies, but it is the basic unit of all societies. It is wonderfully resilient and has withstood the pressures of war, political maneuvering, antifamily logic and attacks from some who want society to adopt policies of free and open sexual encounter. The family is our greatest source of pleasure, support and survival. It is a very large part of God's plan for salvation from loneliness.

5

Mate

"Therefore a man leaves his father
and his mother and cleaves to
his wife, and they become one flesh."
Genesis 2:24

THERE ARE PRESENTLY ABOUT 59 million unmarried adults
in the United States. That is approximately one-third of the
adult population. In twelve years, from 1970 to 1982, the
number increased by 78 per cent. The total number includes those who have never been married (54 per cent),
divorced people (18 per cent), separated spouses (5 per
cent), and widowed men and women (22 per cent). Of the
total, 25 million are men, and nearly 34 million women.[1]
The number of those who have never been married
is growing. Young people are choosing to marry later in
life or not at all. Sociologist Amitai Etzioni says that if
present trends continued "at the same accelerating rate,
by the year 2008, there would not be a single American
family left."[2]
The several million in this country who have never
married could be divided into two categories: those who
have chosen not to marry, and those whose circumstances

have prevented them from marrying.

Many choose not to marry for several reasons. Some will not because it seems too great a risk. Everywhere they see homes breaking up and people suffering. Others will not because of a desire to be independent. Unmarried, they can use their time and money as they please, go where they want and do what they wish with no strings attached. Increasing numbers seem to be joining this group.

Two things fuel the growth of this lifestyle of independence. Affluence is the first, making it possible to lead an extremely interesting life alone, one filled with possessions and travel and a wide range of experiences. The second is the change in attitude toward sexuality and sexual connections outside marriage. With society more open to recreational sex without permanent commitment, the drive to marry has lessened.

With its great concern for self-fulfillment, its lack of commitment to others and its failure to recognize the lordship of Christ, this is a distinctly non-Christian lifestyle.

Many who have been divorced are remaining single for the same reasons. For example, a 37-year-old divorcee who is a federal employee living near Washington says of her choice to remain single, "I can do what I want, when I want, as I want. The only constraints are those I impose on myself."[3] It's my belief that this lifestyle will lead to a great deal of loneliness, if not immediately, at least in the later years of life.

Of course not all who wish to be single are trying to escape commitment, and many are quite willing to abstain from sexual enjoyment and live responsible lives within the context of singleness. Some choose to do so out of devotion to God. In the same way that some are single to serve themselves, others are single to serve God and others.

Gary Collins has presented a collection of essays under the title *It's O.K. To Be Single*. I agree. It *is* O.K. There should be no stigma, no penalty, no suspicion. Singleness is a viable option for the Christian or anyone else.

But if singleness is a viable option, how can it be true that "It is not good for man or woman to be alone"? After all, isn't that the biblical premise of this book?

As I understand this verse of Scripture, it is not saying that singleness is bad on any *moral* grounds. There is nothing morally wrong with living alone as long as one doesn't do so out of immoral and self-centered motives. Rather, I believe God said that being alone is not good because it is difficult and painful for most people, and because the sexes complement each other by propagating the race, fulfilling mutual needs and jointly reflecting the image of God.

There *are* problems with being single. Whether these problems are greater than the problems of being married depends on the needs and sensibilities of the individual. Certainly each Christian is free to choose as the Lord leads. In 1 Corinthians 7:36, Paul speaks of the question of marriage and says, "Let them marry—it is no sin." And two verses later he places his stamp of approval on singleness by saying, "he who marries . . . does well; and he who refrains from marriage will do better."

But we have said nothing about the second category, those who are single not because they want to be but because their circumstances force it upon them. They want to marry. They want a mate and believe that they have God's permission to marry. But because they have never found the right person or because of some personal problem that prevents them from marrying, they remain single. What is the answer to loneliness for these people? Is it legitimate for them actually to search for a mate?

The Legitimate Pursuit
This ad appeared in *Intro,* a magazine called "The Single's Source for Single People."

Eureka. How about a traditional values woman (sans hang-ups) in tune with the '80s. You'll find me warm, gentle, sensuous, capable . . . and great fun. I'm either beautiful or great looking (depending on your taste), 41, 5 ft. 8 in., slim, blond/blue, classy, smart, spiritually healthy and intellectually curious, . . . well-read, . . . well-traveled. . . . Most of all, please share my belief that "commitment" does not mean loss of anything. Los Angeles or anywhere you are.[4]

Now that's one kind of pursuit. The ad is sexually provocative, reflecting the moral flavor of our day. According to *Time* magazine, it soon paid off in a new relationship for the woman who placed it. Even if the ad lacked the promiscuous tone, we could still say that such a method of finding a spouse is risky at best. Without a social context (school, church, neighborhood and so on) the respondant is an unknown quantity.

Taking the opposite approach, some Christians feel that if God wants you to marry, he will bring the right person to your doorstep without any personal effort on anyone's part. Yet I doubt that it's wrong to do a little searching. I think of the journey made by Abraham's servants to find a wife for Isaac. It was a legitimate quest. And it would seem to teach several things. First, God doesn't forbid one's trying to find a mate. Second, God himself will guide the search. And third, such a search ought to be made among those who are fit for Christian marriage.

If one is going to search for a mate, there are some important things worth noting. First a danger: if marriage is the all-consuming goal, and if all one's energies are spent in searching, the quest will devour all the other good things in life. All the information one may gather and enjoy, all the fulfillment one may have, all the completeness and joy possible in the single life can be consumed in the restlessness and discontent of a quest that goes desperately on and on.

The second thing to observe is that many single people "put life on hold," treading water because they are certain they must marry before life can begin. They seem to feel that all that goes before matrimony is prelude, nothing but overture to the performance of the play. So they establish no permanent home, fail to learn to enjoy life independently and put down no roots. This is not fair to God, to the others in one's life, nor to oneself. This attitude is a guarantee that one's best work will never be done and that one's loneliness will grow and grow beyond manageability. Go ahead and live!

The third thing to notice if one is going to search is that most folk find their mates, not by placing ads nor by going to singles' gatherings, but by being brought into contact with others in the normal course of an active life. I am told that singles' bars are a big thing these days. But singles' places of any kind seem to have a built-in problem. The relationships that develop there often have only a thin crust beneath them as a foundation. This thin crust is the mutual desire to find someone, and that really isn't much to have in common. In order to develop intimacy, two people need to share values, commitments, interests and backgrounds—at least that is the ideal. Robert Weiss says that it's risky business to act "outside of one's social context and meet others who are acting outside theirs."[5] One danger is that it tends to "facilitate sexual adventure," whereas meeting others in one's own social context gives "both support and constraint in the relationships ordinarily maintained with kin, friends, co-workers, neighbors, and the others who people one's relational life."[6]

Thes best way to find a mate, then, is to lead an active life in a community of people where there are some unmarried Christians of the opposite sex. Reach out and involve yourself with others through work, worship, recreation and service.

One more thing about a legitimate search: it seems good to me if one can be physically attractive. I understand that not every woman can be beautiful nor every man handsome; rather I am defending the idea that a pleasant appearance is desirable. Every kind of creature in the zoological world has qualities of appearance that draw members of the opposite sex. Human beings are certainly no exception to this, for God did not intend for the race to die out. I think it is quite unrealistic for Christians to suggest that it is somehow unspiritual and improper to give attention to personal beauty.

We speak of a handsome man or a beautiful woman as being "attractive." God made the physiology of the sexes to do exactly that, *attract*. A man's initial interest in a woman is often her face or form, and the same is true of her first notice of him. To ignore this fact in the interest of "spirituality" or because of some idea that it is demeaning to either sex seems a bit foolish to me.

Of course we know that at present our response to physical beauty is overemphasized by the entertainment and advertising media. And there is a difference between taking proper pleasure in being attractive and being vain about one's appearance. But the basic drive to be attractive is so universal that it probably has a biological basis. It certainly has survival value for the individual and for the race. Attention to personal appearance is not sinister so long as it is kept in balance. One may make the best of what one has without feeling guilty about it.

Of course physical beauty is not everything. There are inner qualities that are more important than the external ones, qualities of personality that we will discuss more fully in chapter eight. If we have these inner qualities and also give attention to our personal appearance, it is more likely that someone will want to brighten his or her personal landscape by making us a permanent part of it. Even if one is physically unattractive, personality can more than make up for it.

On the other hand, for some the search for a mate is not possible, and for others it is unproductive. Eventually one may realize that he or she is most likely to be single for the remainder of this life. Singleness may be permanent. In this case what can be done to escape loneliness?

There are a great many who have developed lives of fullness and joy without marriage. They feel no loss, no deprivation. They are interested in people and things around them, and they pursue life with verve and contentment. Singleness is not a sentence to solitary confinement. Rather, it is an opportunity for ministry and a diversity of relationships. The key to joy in singleness is the ability to reach out to others energetically. We will look further at some ways to overcome the loneliness of singleness when we look at the situations of people who were formerly married and are now single.

Divorced People
Of the 59 million single adults in the United States, 18 per cent have been married and are now divorced.[7] Divorce is almost always an experience in loneliness. When severe, long-term tension exists in marriage, divorce brings relief from pain and is therefore quite welcome. But even so, the loss of one's partner produces great loneliness with a special set of problems.

Once there was someone in the house; now it is empty. Perhaps beloved children are gone too. There is an empty bed, the absence of touch, no one to talk to in that special way. The loneliness is more intense than for the never-married, because in many cases the divorced person has tasted, at least for a short time, the wine of true intimacy. No matter how far apart the two had grown before their permanent separation, it still may be possible for them to remember the good days when they loved and shared, when they gave each other wholehearted support, found joy in each other's embrace and had every confidence that they would grow old together.

Now for each of them the separate workloads are borne alone. There is an empty place at the table, a house totally still at night or an impersonal apartment that is not home. There is no one to touch in the same way, no one who can listen so well to the problems of the day, no one with whom to share its pleasantness.

Divorce is the death not only of a relationship, but also of ideals, dreams and aspirations. For the Christian it is an even greater defeat. The Lord's plan for our lives has not been carried out; our Christian testimony is soiled.

But there is more. If there are children, someone will care for them without the regular help of the mate who is their natural parent. He or she will likely suffer to see the pain they feel at the end of family unity.

In addition, there is no one to whom to express one's love in a sexual way. The loss of sexual intimacy will be acutely felt.

Then there are the social problems that may come as a complete surprise. Besides the loss of one's partner, old friends and old group relationships are also lost. Those who loved you both will tend to take sides and lay blame on one or the other. Neither partner will feel comfortable in the group of couples that the two enjoyed together, and the group itself will feel awkward to the point that they may no longer invite either to their social gatherings. Even if they do not condemn you, they will certainly feel ill at ease around you.

This means that some of the major resources that once kept one from being lonely are now gone right when they are needed most. Even the church may cease to be a resource. Since divorce is an act against the sanctity of the home and therefore against God's creation, Christian friends may be among the first to turn and walk away. Certainly there are Christians who are sensitive and compassionate. These will realize that they cannot stand as judges and that they do not really know the pressures that drove the two apart. With wise and good Christian friends, a divorced person can continue to see the church as a resource. But sadly, that is not always true.

The divorced person has one more special problem in loneliness. The never-married person can hope to find a mate someday, and the widowed can hope to marry again, but remarriage is somewhat less likely for the divorced person on several counts. First, if the person is a Christian, he or she may believe that remarriage is wrong. Much has been written on that topic in recent years—whether Scripture permits remarriage, and if it does, under what circumstances. I will not enter that discussion in this book. But if one decides that remarriage is forbidden, then a significant avenue for fighting loneliness is closed. Remarriage is also unlikely if the person is embittered toward the opposite sex, or if having once failed, he or she lacks courage to try again.

At the very least, this advice is appropriate: don't shut yourself away! Personal well-being depends largely on the ability and drive to establish social relationships that will keep a person alive spiritually, intellectually and emotionally.

If the old social network fails you, enter a new one. If the church you were a part of is no longer warm and open to you, either stay with it until the barriers fall, or find a new one. This is easy to say and difficult to do, but there are fine Bible-believing groups that will not shut you away.

The Widowed
In the autumn of 1982, Ariel Durant died at the age of 83.

She was the wife of Will Durant, the leading popular historian of the twentieth century, the "biographer of Mankind." Will and Ariel had met when he was a 27-year-old instructor and she a 14-year-old student. Her real name was Ida, but because of her liveliness and verve he renamed her.

The two loved each other and flew in the face of convention to marry. For sixty-eight years they lived and worked together, coauthoring the monumental eleven volume, ten-thousand-page work, *The Story of Civilization.*[8]

Only thirteen days after Ariel died, Will Durant died also. It isn't at all unusual for two who have lived and loved for so long together to die within a short space of time. There are husbands and wives so close that it seems their lives are bound up in the same bundle, and when one is gone, the other cannot continue to live.

I realize that it is not always so. Some grow so far apart that the going of the one is no great loss to the other. Still others are deeply devoted, and when one dies the other has no wish to go on living, yet many years of life remain.

A couple I knew well lived and worked together hand in hand from their youth. They had many wonderful memories and were completely dedicated to each other's mutual happiness. Ernest died at the age of 74. Lydia wanted to die immediately and often talked of when she would go to join him. The Sunday after his passing, her eyes misted with tears, she told me that she had not wanted to go to church. Then she smiled and said, "But then I remembered that this was Ernest's first Sunday in heaven, and I just couldn't stay home!" Though the adjustment to his being gone was very difficult, Lydia lived for many more years after Ernest's death.

Of the 59 million single adults in our country, 22 per cent are widowed.[9] Some of these are young, but most are older, and widowed women over 65 outnumber widowed men of the same age six to one.

Loss of a spouse brings many difficulties. Sometimes there is unaccountable resentment toward the deceased mate, almost as though he or she died intentionally. A good friend of ours who is nearly eighty lost her husband about ten years ago. Theirs had been one of those storybook marriages, and they absolutely adored each other.

Recently she told me with a chuckle how she had wanted to celebrate their forty-fifth wedding anniversary. He disliked such celebrations, so they compromised and planned a more elaborate fiftieth anniversary observance. But before the five years were up, he died. She said, "We were going to have a big celebration, and he just up and left! I was so provoked with him!"

But in a much more serious vein, she struggled with overwhelming loneliness after he was gone. Part of it had to do with her realization that she had reached the end of the golden age of her own life. "We had such a wonderful marriage, and suddenly it hit me that it was over and I would never have another relationship like that ever again in this life. When I realized that, I just screamed and screamed in the agony of it!"

Time has passed, and this dear woman has adjusted well, has great numbers of friends, remains very active, loves her present life and wants to continue to live as long as possible.

But many react differently, and some are even permanently debilitated by their loss. Interviews with twenty-two widowed women drew these comments: "I never stop missing him." "I keep seeing his very fair hair and the color of his eyes." "I can see him, quite vividly, coming in the door." "I can almost feel his skin and touch his hands." Some of these women would see their husband's face on a stranger coming down the street or think that a car was his and that he was driving it. Others would hear the door open and close as he "came in," wake to his call in the night, or talk to him and expect an answer. They were often drawn to places where they had once gone together.[10]

For some, widowhood is the beginning of the loss of health. C. S. Lewis married while in his fifties. He and his wife, Joy, seemed a perfect match, and they reveled in each other in every way. Lewis remarked to a friend, "I never expected to have in my sixties, the happiness that passed me by in my twenties."[11]

But in 1960, Joy died of cancer. Lewis's American friend Chad Walsh said, "Lewis never really recovered from the loss of Joy. When I next saw him in late 1961, he was subdued and at loose ends. His own health had begun to fail. . . . He had been a man of tremendous zest during most of his life, but toward the end I think he was ready for death."[12] Lewis died just a little over three years after Joy's passing.

He had cried out in the pain of loneliness, "Oh God, God, why did you take such trouble to force this creature out of its shell if it is now doomed to crawl back—to be sucked back—into it?"[13]

Defenses against Loneliness

It's time to turn our attention to solutions, to defenses against mate-loneliness. The things I will say here apply broadly to those who have never married and to the divorced and widowed.

First, *one has to accept what cannot be changed.* This is hard advice that no one wants to take. But if, in spite of all efforts to find a mate, you find none, if remarriage after divorce is not acceptable or possible, if you lose your mate at a stage of life that prevents you from taking another, come to terms with that fact.

My friend who wanted the anniversary celebration realized that the finest relationship of her life had ended and could not be duplicated. She was honest with herself, grieved over her situation and gradually came to terms with it. The permanent loss, the closed door, was accepted, and she went forward with the business of living. With acceptance came activity, travel, the enjoyment of old acquaintances, spiritual deepening and intellectual inquiry.

I do not say that she is no longer lonely for her lost mate. I'm sure she is. But she has triumphed by growing, and life is worth living in spite of her loss and her age.

Next, *refuse to retreat into a shell.* A grand, permanent withdrawal as an act of grief and desolation solves nothing. There are too many people to come to know—people who need your companionship, people who can make life worthwhile—to hide away in undying grief.

Be realistic about the grass on the other side. I have never believed we should lie to ourselves in order to feel better about anything like Aesop's fox who couldn't reach the grapes. Finally he gave up and went away, saying to himself, "Oh well, they were probably sour anyway!"

On the other hand, those grapes *may* have been sour. A realistic appraisal will often tell us that the thing we want so badly may not be as sweet as we think. Here I am thinking of those who wish to marry or remarry.

Marriage looks like a wonderful solution to everything, and when it is good it does solve many problems. But when it is bad it solves nothing and, indeed, creates a whole new world of problems and agonies. Someone has said, "There is nothing quite so miserable as being alone, unless it's wishing that you were."

A man I went to college with was married for twelve years and has been divorced for about four. He told me that life with his former wife was a daily agony. He said he told the Lord that if the marriage could be ended he would be glad to be single for the rest of his life. True to his word, he has not remarried and is not keeping company with anyone who might be a prospective wife. He is celibate and tells me he has never been happier. I expect a good bit of his happiness is based on the fact that he has something with which to compare his present state.

I don't say this to encourage anyone to divorce or separate, but to illustrate that being alone is better than being tied to a very difficult mate. There are countless couples who wish most earnestly that they had never married.

Marriage is intended to provide companionship, but often it only yokes two people who were once compatible and are now antagonists. Marriage is intended to give sexual joy. But the truth is that many married men and women are ignored by their partners until they burn not only with sexual desire, but also with flames of resentment at the other's lack of compassion and withered sexuality.

Marriage should provide security. Yet a single person may have far more ability to lay up resources for old age than a person who is attached to a prodigal mate.

Realizing these things may help one make peace with singleness!

Another defense against loneliness is to realize that there are advantages to being single, that these advantages can be accepted as a gift and then enjoyed. One writer points out that if you live alone you can do as you please. You can get up in the middle of the night to play records. You don't have to pick up your socks or shoes or anything else. You may plan a vacation without consulting anyone and take off at a moment's notice. "The bathroom is all yours, every day, all the time."

I have some problems with this approach. Without a good bit of tempering, it is altogether too self-centered. A married friend of mine finds it quite attractive. He noted with envy that a single friend of his can buy what he wants when he wants it. Then he added, "Sometimes I wish I were single so I could get some things I want."

There is something very wrong in being glad to give up a wholesome human relationship in favor of a lifestyle or a relationship to an object.

I would *not* say to the single person: "Look at what you can have and do if you remain single!" What I would say is that if marriage does not develop, or if you must live alone, then the freedom you have to come and go, to have and do, can be welcomed as a consolation.

Have confidence in God's plan. I don't know whether God has a specific will for you in regard to marriage or not. But you can be certain that God can bring good out of your singleness. Romans 8:28 assures you of that.

Cultivate thankfulness. all that we have—our very breath, all the good things we enjoy—is a gift of grace. Make an intelligent choice here. Rather than chafing against your circumstances, rather than lusting for what God has not made possible, be grateful for what he has given you. To do that you must concentrate on the fact that all good things are undeserved gifts which provide happiness that we did not earn.

G. K. Chesterton said, "Joy . . . is the gigantic secret of the Christian." When we have joy in what we do and what we have, we adjust well no matter how formidable our circumstances. To have this joy we must take the time and make the effort to relish what we have. Taste the present gift. Allow yourself to be filled with ecstasy by seeing the light in the eye of a child, the smile on a friend's face, the blue of the sky, or any evidence that with every rising of the sun, God's mercies are made new to us (Lam 2:22).

Refuse to accept the idea that you are treading water or marking time. We spoke of this dangerous attitude earlier in the chapter. It is to be avoided at all costs. Go ahead and give yourself permission to live!

And as you live, *have a well-defined goal for life.* Goals are for the young and the aged. God's glory should be just as important to the ninety-year-old as to one who is nineteen.

Not long ago a Christian near her nineties said to me, "I don't know why God doesn't just go ahead and let me die.

I'm not any use to anybody." Her infirmities were making life very difficult for her, but I answered by pointing out how much her children, grandchildren, and great-grand-children love her. It seems to her that she's of no value, but they need her as an object of their attention and love. Even if all one is able to do is sit and receive the love of others, it can be done with joy.

Having said this, I am painfully aware that there are those who have no one to shower love and attention on them. But most of us are able to find someone if we try. Finding someone, doing something for him or her, letting the Lord love another through you will give a sense of worth, which is important in combating loneliness. Whatever your goal, strive to reach your full capacity in meeting it.

Reach out for friends. Do this by being part of the community in which you live. As I suggested in chapter four, attach yourself to a family. If you are young and your natural family is halfway across the continent or around the world, you can develop a relationship with another family that will love you and be a great help to you and you to them. Jesus said something that speaks to this need. He said, "And every one who has left houses or brothers or sisters or father or mother or children or lands, for my name's sake, will receive a hundredfold, and inherit eternal life" (Mt 19:29).

Develop the ability to care and accept the love of another in return. No one who really cares for someone and is cared for by that person in return can be fully lonely.

Be careful to maintain your physical health. Health is an advantage against loneliness. Sluggishness of body contributes to sluggishness of mind and spirit and subsequently to the low emotional state in which we are so vulnerable.

Be certain of your own value. When a divorce occurs or when one wishes to be married but can find no one, there is almost certain to be a sense of lost value. "Why did my mate leave me?" "Am I so undesirable that no one is interested in me?" "I must be a worthless person." This is a normal fruit of rejection.

If we can realize that we really do have substantial value, our emotional battle will be won more easily. To realize this, we must see that value doesn't depend on the work we do, the activities in which we engage or the people who accept or reject us. Each of us has value apart from these things.

Value and identity are not the same. I can identify myself as a particular person by saying that I am a white male in my forties, a Christian, a pastor, married, a father. I can give my name, my social security number, and say that my hair is black and graying, that I am a bit overweight and that I have a passion for certain hobbies, writing and family life. With a photograph one could pick me out of a crowd; that is, one could identify me.

Yet I can know all of that about myself and still feel empty and alone. What I need to give me a sense of fullness is the belief that I have not only identity but also value. But if value does not come from the things that identify me, where does it come from? It comes from some person outside myself. For nothing has value unless someone wants it.

You will say, "That's my very problem. Nobody wants me!" But it isn't correct to say that no one wants you. Let me elaborate. Antique stores don't place big prices on objects no one wants. The greater the public desire for an object, the more they can charge for it. And in the last analysis, *an object is worth whatever someone is willing to pay for it.* If a millionaire falls in love with a lamp and is able to persuade its owner to part with it for a quarter million dollars, and if the millionaire gives that much for it, then no matter what someone else would have paid, that lamp is worth a quarter million dollars. The highest price the millionaire is willing to give is its value.

Our value is determined the same way. God gave Christ

for you. How valuable is God's Son? We cannot possibly imagine any upward limit on Jesus' value. Don't you see, then, that your value has been determined already? It is derived from *God's* desire. Your value is established for all time by what he gave to redeem you, his Son. If you can take hold of that, then you will feel a great sense of security. This security will be a strength to you in the face of any rejection and in the absence of any particular relationship, even in the absence of a mate.

6

Intimacy and Romance

"I feel I am your double,
Like you outside, in dark.
I cannot draw the line
Dividing you from me."
Boris Pasternak, "Meeting"

I HAVE HEARD THAT ROMANTIC love is an invention of the recent past, that when our great-grandfathers courted our great-grandmothers, their aims were strictly utilitarian. Grandpa wanted a good strong woman to produce his children and keep his house in order. He wanted lots of children because the more he had, the more land he could farm and the lighter his own load would be. Life was a matter-of-fact sort of thing, and a wife was a good person to have around because she helped get things done.

Now I'm sure that some men have looked at marriage like that, and I expect some still do. But all in all, that seems a pretty cynical view to me. Isn't it true that from the dawn of recorded history there have been men and women who have loved each other in a tender, devoted, idealistic way? Hasn't there always been more to marriage than utilitarianism?

Look at the record we have in literature. The ancients enjoyed reading about love. Poetry from the ancient Chinese, tragedies from Greece, epic poetry from the earliest written English and the best of today's writings include tales of genuine affection between men and women. From Euripides to Shakespeare to Pasternak, the sexes have loved each other in a romantic way.

I believe that this is a basic need showing through, that human beings have always longed to have one person who is very near and who in a unique way is his or hers alone. I believe that we wish to be part of a whole which is created by bringing two people of complementary personalities together, a whole that reflects God in his diversity with both masculine and feminine virtues, virtues which exist beyond the concept of sex and which existed first in him. This is the ideal for marriage.

So in the beginning God created humanity in his own image, male and female, an entity to project his character into the world. In this creation story we find the root of intimacy between the sexes, the root of human mating; the root that has given rise to, but transcended physical desire.

When we speak of a mate we are talking about someone very close. "My mate," we say, one who belongs to me in a way that he or she belongs to no one else. A possession who possesses me. The word also speaks of completeness. "Where is the mate to this shoe?" we ask, or this glove, this swan, this man, this woman. Yet even within this supposedly completed state, loneliness can grow where intimacy does not.

Adam's Joy

When God observed that it was not good for the man to be alone, he brought the beasts of the world to him. In a review of all living things Adam found no one to be his helper. Perhaps he felt cheated. Then God caused a deep sleep to fall on him and from Adam's body took a rib. From the rib he created woman and brought her to Adam.

There are two words in the Genesis account which we consistently overlook. These two words tell us a great deal about Adam's feeling when he first saw Eve. I think they reveal the frustration that he felt after the long, fruitless search. Even more they reveal the desire he had for his own mate, and they reflect Eve's perfect ability to meet his lonely condition.

The two words are "at last"! With a great rush of pleasure and joy he sees her for the first time and says, "This *at last* is bone of my bones and flesh of my flesh" (Gen 2:23). In the midst of perfection, longing for something more, the animals not having satisfied his need, he is ecstatic with God's creation of a perfect mate for him.

The words are filled with surprise. Never before had he seen any creature like himself. How hard this is for us to imagine! In all the animal kingdom there had been nothing so like him as she.

His words are filled with the sweet perfume of intimacy—"bone of my bones . . . flesh of my flesh"—and they reflect nearness, affection and security. The biblical account is given from Adam's vantage point, but Eve must surely have found as much pleasure in Adam as he found in her. It was a mutually fulfilling relationship.

We do not live in Eden. Yet the ideal of Eden remains in our minds. When we think of marriage we tend to dream of a marriage like the one Adam and Eve had before the Fall. But this is an illusion. No one could ever meet the standard of these two lovers as they loved before the world fell into ruin. Yet it is to our benefit, as well as to our sorrow, that we long for Eden's perfection. In some marriages the ideal is very nearly attained, and when this happens, marriage produces the greatest joy and happiness that one can know on earth. When the marriage does not come near this ideal, the husband or wife may feel incomplete despite the married state.

Lonely in Marriage

There are two basic ways to have a lonely marriage. Two people can be married to each other and yet be lonely because there is an emotional division of some sort between them. They live together, share the same bedroom, eat at the same table, have the same friends and raise the same children, yet they are emotionally divorced.

The other way is to have actual physical separation in spite of great love for each other. One's mate travels on business, is away at war or is confined to prison. Another kind of physical separation is due not to distance, but to bodily illness. One of the partners is no longer able to participate in life normally, perhaps is unable to communicate at all. We are probably all acquainted with some couple, one of whom has Alzheimer's disease or muscular dystrophy, has suffered a stroke or has some other debilitating illness. Often we marvel at the well partner's devotion in faithfulness and care. We see one of the true mountain peaks of love. Yet we know that there is a sense of loss and loneliness among those separated from a partner through illness.

An elderly woman I know faithfully attended to her husband's needs following a stroke that left him an invalid. Shortly after he died we were talking together about her adjustment to widowhood. She said, "I'm adjusting very well. After all, Will's been gone for over a year now." He had died less than a week before, but months ago the stroke had taken the Will she had always known and loved.

But now let's turn our attention to the first kind of separation in marriage, the kind that comes from painful emotional division. Remember that loneliness is a state of mind, and that it is possible to be in a crowd and yet be lonely. The same holds true for mate-loneliness. It is possible to be married and living with one's partner, and yet be lonely.

When two people stand together at the marriage altar they normally have a deep emotional nearness and believe that they will answer each other's needs. Each feels that a good mate has been found. But after a time many couples find themselves walking divergent paths and eventually come to feel that, though they are married, they are not at all mates. When this happens, loneliness follows.

Loneliness of this kind is one of the most miserable of all varieties. Someone is near, yet not near. The two can no longer reach each other, though they need each other as much as they ever did. This terrible misery is at its worst for the sensitive person who really wants companionship but is rebuffed in all efforts to attain it. It is awful for the lover to be rejected by the beloved. This kind of rejection is so horrible that in the book of Hosea, God himself uses an instance of it to illustrate the way in which the human race has rejected him.

Jeanne Hendricks, author of *A Woman for All Seasons,* was discussing with friends the loneliness singles feel during holiday seasons. A woman spoke up and said, "Yes, but there is something worse: being together with someone who isn't really with you—that's loneliness."[1]

Somehow we all sense that a great many marriages are like that. Legally and in the eyes of God, the two are partners. But emotionally they are isolated from each other, living in a union that is a hollow shell. Some reach the extreme in which they no longer respect each other, no longer want one another's company nor even wish each other well.

How does it happen? Many things can set the two on their ever-widening paths. A husband may be work-bound with no time for his wife. Or it may be the wife's workload that leaves the husband alone, for women too can become just as absorbed by their careers as their male counterparts.

Often one partner runs off and leaves the other intellectually. Many a young woman has worked hard to put her husband through college, only to find that study and intellectual involvement has opened up a new world to him that they cannot share.

Emotional separation may develop because one of the two is a romantic and the other is incurably practical. By *romantic* I mean one who dreams, feels deeply and is sensitive to the colors and joys of life. This kind of person often has a deeper than ordinary appreciation for the pleasures of sharing with a mate. And when a romantic is married to one who is insensitive to these joys, no matter how good and stable the unromantic partner may be, the romantic is likely to begin to pine after what he or she considers the indispensable elements of love.

Other situations may create loneliness in marriage. One partner may have an inquiring mind while the other does not. One may have strong sexual drives while the other lacks sexual interest. One may be warm and touching, the other coolly distant. One may be noncompetitive, wanting only a loving sense of equality, while the other feels compelled to prove personal superiority. One may be absorbed in friends and interests outside the family while the other is family oriented. One may be pleasant, loving peace and harmony, the other combative. One may be spiritually alive, the other not concerned with God at all. One may be dominant and directive, while the other does not wish to be dominated. One may long for wealth and social status, while the other is content with a simple lifestyle. One may wish for a feeling of mutual belonging, the other be fiercely independent.

Another important cause of emotional division is the desire of one or both partners to receive more than they are willing to give. This is another example of the excessive individualism Louise Bernikow described: "We want independence *and* a faithful lover, we want the support of family but not its demands."[2] Perry London, professor of psychology and psychiatry at the University of Southern California, says that the sexual revolution has made marriage "an extension of the playmate and friendship arrangements in childhood, in which the sharing of interests and affection do not imply any bonds of mutual obligation."[3]

If that is true, then one can easily see why marriages fail so often today. Without commitment of a permanent kind, without a sense of mutual belonging, it isn't possible to meet a partner's needs. No wonder there is anger in so many marriages. Spouses feel neglected and shortchanged. I recently heard a young woman say to her husband, "I don't belong to you or to anyone else! I want to be your friend, but I don't *belong* to you!" Their conversation ended there. She was angry and he was hurt. He *wanted* to belong to her, and he wanted to feel that she was his. Her outburst left him feeling quite alone.

No matter what its cause, loneliness in marriage is a very serious problem. The lonely one often becomes preoccupied with personal misery. It is as though a dense fog has settled upon the mind, and the person thinks of little else. He or she feels deprived and victimized. If the lonely person has a romantic nature, his or her heart may begin to yearn for companionship until it bleeds. Ballads of lost love that went unnoticed before now become theme songs. Sunlight playing on the shimmering leaves of cottonwood and aspen seem to be singing bittersweet songs of love not yet found.

Sounds silly, doesn't it? Foolishly romantic. Yes, but the sensitive person, pressed hard by an ideal but prevented by a distant and unresponsive mate from attaining it, is likely to think such things and to dream irresponsible dreams. To the afflicted these things are real, and they are overwhelming.

Often the result of loneliness in marriage is tragic. The sensitive, emotionally isolated person begins to say, "This is unfair! I have such a need for warmth, affection and companionship. And I have so much love to give and could make some empty person so happy." This person is in the midst of a great emotional and moral storm. It is easy to see that this is the stuff of which sin is made.

When pain exists it is only natural to want to escape it. The lonely partner may plead for greater sensitivity from his or her spouse, but if the spouse doesn't respond, and if the lonely one cannot find a way to escape the pain or to be responsible in spite of it, then the end of the marriage may be in sight.

The unresponsive one comes to be thought of as a roadblock, the one who "forces me to be lonely," the one thing preventing the formation of a genuine attachment with someone more suitable. The lonely one may even begin to fantasize about the partner's death. But death doesn't come, and step by step the rationalizations necessary to divorce are made. Principles once thought inviolable are shattered. The obstructive partner is removed and the lonely one goes on down the road, free to search for the illusive ideal.

Mate-related loneliness is an opportunity for sin. Yet let us be fair. Who would not sympathize with such misery? Who would refuse to understand? Who would have no compassion? After all, did not God create us with the capacity for such feelings? Did not he himself say that it is not good to be alone? And such a one certainly is alone in a most miserable way. The Fall, human sinfulness, deprived the lonely partner of legitimate fulfillment. Doesn't the blame lie with the Fall? Isn't the old partner's unresponsiveness just as sinful as the subsequent infidelity?

In a sense all of that is true. We cannot leave the matter there, however. There is still a deeper word to say, and that deeper word is *responsibility*.

Society has a need that is greater than the individual's need for fulfillment. That need is for responsible marriage partners. If we are to contribute to the social order, to the emotional balance of children, to living out the gospel, to glorifying God and to showing Christ to the world, we must care more about being responsible than about being fulfilled. That is not an easy standard to attain in today's fantasy-filled world. Yet when it is attained, true responsibility will cause us to make personal sacrifice when necessary in order to keep marriage intact.

What Will Ease These Feelings?

Suppose that rather than escaping a marriage in which there is loneliness, one decides to be responsible, even though the uncaring mate will not change. Are there solutions that will ease the feelings of isolation? Not instantly, I'm afraid. The answer is in growth. Of course counseling is available to those in such straits, and it is possible to divert oneself by wholeheartedly entering endeavors and projects worthy of the energies once devoted to the goal of self-fulfillment. Beyond that I will have to be satisfied by saying that every Christian should make it a goal of life to become a good mate, one who can fulfill the needs that his or her partner may have. This will lay the foundation for dealing with the loneliness by focusing on a goal outside oneself rather than on inner pain.

We can also be strengthened by taking some steps. First, we must reaffirm our Christian commitment to marriage as a God-given union, and we must reaffirm our commitment to being responsible. This will lay the foundation for dealing with the loneliness itself.

·Second, we must review the marriage partner's good qualities, dwelling on them until we can be genuinely thankful. It is true that some have faults so serious and so detrimental to one's own life or to the life of one's children that no good quality can offset them. For example, a father who sexually assaults his children should not be tolerated. But in most cases, the good outweighs the bad, and thankfulness rather than rejection is in order.

Third, we must refuse to allow resentment to build. Resentment drives couples apart and brings bitterness. There are some things Christians can do to prevent resentment. We can pray. That is basic. God really can make vital differences in us as we bring our burdens to him. We can also find someone to talk to about our loneliness—perhaps a wise friend whose life is in good order, perhaps a pastor or a professional marriage counselor. (But I would warn you against choosing a nonprofessional of the opposite sex. Unknown to you, his or her problem may be the same as yours, and you may begin to see each other as the mutual solution.) Then, having found the right confidant, ventilate. Talk it out. Receive good counsel and put it into action. Also, prevent the build-up of resentment through forgiveness. Usually our own failures are as great or greater than those of our partner, and we expect to be forgiven both by God and our fellow men and women. Forgiveness is basic to every relationship that the Christian has. We should learn it and practice it well.

Fourth, we need to build on the good we have discovered in our partner. Accept him or her and work for harmony.

Joy in Diversity
This fourth step in combating loneliness in marriage is to realize that diverse interests do not necessarily mean we are mismatched.

Hannah Lee, in her book *Help Your Husband Stay Alive*, tells of a friend who became aware of a great many differences between herself and her husband. The more she thought about them the more important they seemed.

However, they had one strong similarity. They were wonderfully compatible sexually and frequently engaged in joyous, spontaneous lovemaking.

One day she said to her husband, "We really haven't a thing in common but sex, have we?" He responded, "I guess that's right." "But that can't be enough, can it?" she asked. He looked at her with sudden wonder. "More than enough," he said gently and ate his breakfast and went off to work.[4] The wife recognized the truth of this and was able to continue to enjoy her marriage.

Having offered that story as an illustration, I am still very much aware that for many a good sexual relationship is not enough fulfillment to prevent loneliness. The point I wish to make is that we often expect too much, and we fail to emphasize the similarities that we do have. If we can emphasize the similarities and value what we have in this person, develop appreciation for the other's interests and allow him or her uncritical freedom to be different from ourselves, we will have taken great strides toward escaping loneliness.

Modifying Expectations
Another important step we can take is to adjust our expectations. If one *must* have the ideal marriage, if one *expects* it, then he or she is most likely to wind up without any marriage at all. Strive for the best, but learn to be content with less than the ideal. And I do mean content! Not heaving unhappy sighs of resignation, but living in true contentedness that says honestly, "This is good! I'm glad to be in this situation."

Our expectations have a great deal to do with being contented. In fact happiness is largely a function of expectation. It has been observed that men and women who graduate from college expect a higher income. When, in spite of their education, the income does not meet that standard, they are disappointed and unhappy. On the other hand, men and women who graduate from high school often expect less. Though they make no more than the college graduates, they tend to be contented and happy with what they receive because it is more than they had expected.

If we get less than we expect, we tend to be unhappy. If we get more, we tend to be happy. That holds true for marriage. If we expect a pre-Fall ideal, like the pins in a bowling alley we are set up to be knocked down.

Reaching Outside the Home

The last thing I would say about overcoming loneliness in marriage is as important as the rest. Reach out. Don't place the whole load of your personal fulfillment on your partner's shoulders. Develop outside friendships and enjoy them. Of course as a Christian you cannot look for sexual fulfillment outside marriage. If that is what is missing, and if it is a very compelling need for you, then you have a difficult problem that must be dealt with wisely and with restraint.

But the advice does hold. Reach out for good friendships, for compelling interests and for opportunities to serve others. I know that I seem to be counseling sublimation as an answer. And though I tend not to like it, that is exactly what I am doing. But in a fallen world, that is sometimes the best that can be done.

Here, then, are basic ways to combat loneliness in marriage. (1) Reaffirm your Christian commitment to marriage and to responsible behavior. (2) Review and dwell on your partner's good qualities; be thankful for them, and learn to build on them. (3) Refuse to allow resentment to grow. (4) Realize that diverse interests do not mean incompatibility. (5) Adjust your expectations to realistic levels. (6) Reach out to others in order to take the load of fulfillment off your spouse.

I believe that if you have a will to do so, and if you exercise these disciplines faithfully, you can deal successfully with loneliness in marriage.

The Ideal Solution

The best solution for these problems lies in a mutual effort to become warm and responsive to our partner's needs. It really is possible to change, to learn to think in different ways, to begin to hear what our mate is asking for, to take the time to share the joys of life. Few marriages are really fifty-fifty propositions, each partner giving and receiving equally. But if one becomes aware that he or she is receiving more than giving, and that refusal to adjust is causing pain, then it is an unloving thing not to change.

Something very wonderful happens when a man and woman love each other enough to adjust. It is not only wonderful, it is Christlike. It is obedience to his words in John 15:12, "Love one another as I have loved you."

When we work toward intimacy in marriage, we lessen loneliness, increase personal happiness, and cooperate with God who created the vacuum that can only be filled with human intimacy.

7

Community

"By the rivers of Babylon,
There we sat down and wept,
When we remembered Zion.
Upon the willows in the midst of it
We hung our harps. . . .
How can we sing the LORD's song
In a foreign land?"
Psalm 137:1-4 NASB

ON A COLD DECEMBER EVENING Linda, the children and I were visiting friends when we saw a red glow near the western horizon and realized that something was on fire. A telephone call confirmed the location and nature of the blaze. A large barn in which a farmer kept tractors, other machinery and tools was burning. The building was dangerously near the family home. The location was about seven miles away from where we were visiting.

Immediately my friend went to his own barn, brought out a farm truck with a five-hundred-gallon tank on the bed and began to fill it with water. When it was filled and we roared out of the drive and onto the road, my friend said, "All we have out here are our neighbors."

"Out here" is the extreme western part of Kansas, the high plains that rise as they move westward before merging with the foothills of the Rocky Mountains. Here the distance between the houses is substantial. Our own closest neighbors live one and a half miles from our little rural church and parsonage.

That night when we reached the fire, neighbors were everywhere. Other farmers had also brought their water tanks, and fire trucks were pumping the water onto the blaze. Everywhere men and women were working in the bright light of the flaming building and its glowing red walls. And at some point in the evening, almost to a man, each came up to the farmer to lay an arm on his shoulder and tell him how sorry he was at his loss and how glad he was that no one had been hurt.

"All We Have Out Here . . . "

Two things stand out in my memory about that night: the sights and sounds of the people working together in the light of the flames, and my friend's words as we started toward the blaze—"All we have out here are our neighbors." He was right, and they're good to have!

That night brought to my mind another fire. It began on a summer evening in another state. This, too, was in a rural community, but one with a much heavier population and a very different attitude. While again visiting in a home and eating the evening meal we saw a glow. This time the fire was much nearer, and it was soon decided that it was a home in which a husband and wife lived with their children. Having determined where it was, everyone turned again to the food.

"Aren't we going over there?" I asked.

"No. We couldn't do anything if we did."

What Is a Community?

Community is a complex idea. We use the word in varied

ways to mean anything from a geographical area to a body of cooperating nations. It can mean a special-interest group (as in "the oil-producing community") or a political organization. In this chapter I use it to mean the people who live in a common location and who also have some mutual interest in each other.

At its best, the people of a community know each other (sometimes from birth to death); have a mutual affection; interact socially; share joys, sorrows and needs; and give and receive mutual help. To a meaningful degree they share a set of values and goals. The community's value system sets the limits on what is acceptable behavior and keeps a beneficent watch on its members.

I offer that as an ideal, one that really exists, though not everywhere. Frankly, I do not know what determines whether the people who live in a location will possess the qualities of true community. Is it density of population? Where people are few, do they value and trust each other more than where they are like sardines packed in a can? Is there less community in, say, New Jersey, where there are on the average 978 people to the square mile, than in Wyoming, where there are only 4?[1] That may have something to do with it. But on the other hand there may be strong community among the people who live in row houses in our great cities.

Yet it is probably true that where every person is known by every other person folk are more likely to be careful about how they behave. Each one knows the amount of trust he or she can reasonably place in each neighbor, and so there may be less uncertainty, less mistrust, suspicion and fear.

But we can't all live in Wyoming. And while the town or countryside where we live may not *be* a community, I believe it is possible to find a community, or several communities, within its population. More about this later.

A Hedge against Loneliness

When we care for someone who cares for us, we cannot be totally lonely. Caring is what happens in a real community. Therefore, we can say that being part of a community is a strong hedge against loneliness.

Our need for being part of a community is another of those God-given vacuums. It is important to be a member of a group that will come to our rescue in crisis, sympathize in sorrow and be glad at our good fortune; a group into whose social networks we may enter freely and comfortably. We need the simple pleasures that flow from being with others. We need the picnics, the doorstep conversations, the laughter. Not only do we find pleasure in being part of a community, we also find out just who we are. We are a part of this place, these people. The men and women here provide us with models by which we shape our lives. Unconsciously we learn, "This is who I am, and this is what I am supposed to be."

We also find out something about our personal value. We said in chapter five that we find our value in Christ, and that is true. But it is also true that we find part of our value in the community. If the old friends of the family think well of my children, they are more likely to grow up thinking well of themselves. If my community accepts me, acts benevolently toward me, then I will feel that I am a valuable person. Thinking well of myself, I will find it easier to think well of others and reach out to them.

There is a real sense in which, when we choose to settle in one good place, investing our lives there, we are investing in our own emotional stability and in the emotional stability and future happiness of our children and their children after them. We are also investing in the stability of society.

Forces That Work against Community

Several years ago I lived in a metropolitan area of about

three hundred thousand and did not know the family three doors away. While that really was my own fault, there were contributing circumstances.

Then one Sunday morning snow began to fall. By noon movement in the city was seriously hindered, and by evening the area was paralyzed. Nineteen inches of snow had fallen in a city not equipped to deal with so much. For two days no one went anywhere.

On the third day, though vehicles were still stranded, it was possible to get out and walk to the local supermarket to buy groceries. As people met, they smiled at each other. They waved and spoke to those who lived on their own block. At the supermarket men stood out front, leaning against the building or even sitting on their haunches, talking to one another just as their grandfathers had in front of the old neighborhood store two generations before them.

What was different? At least two things. First, no one could meet the usual full schedule of responsibilities and activities. No one was on the way to work, because the offices and factories were closed. Not being in a hurry, people had time for their neighbors. The other difference was that we were all deprived of our mobile steel and glass insulators. Those were all sitting in drifts somewhere. Normally we would go into our garages, enter our autos and move along the streets to our destinations in as private a manner as though we had never left our homes, insulated from everything and everyone.

It is surprising to see how our technology controls our lives. But on this day our technology was bound by soft white walls, and we were free to act like human beings. Two days later the reprieve was over and we sped along in our usual way, absorbed in our own business and insulated from all about us.

Inflexible schedules, hurry, and machines that take us long distances without contact with others—all these decree that if we are to touch and be touched by our neighbors, we will have to put forth extra effort. And this will be the case in towns of 2,000, suburbs of 40,000 and cities of 4 million.

A Problem for American Women

Another thing that militates against community is the rate at which Americans move from one home to another. With one person in five moving every year, it is hard to build communities. It takes time to know those who live about us, to learn the resources of an area, to be trusted and to find one's way into the social network.

Studies have shown that this very thing has often been a major cause of loneliness among American women, although the situation is now changing. In order to move up the corporate ladder, to earn more pay, to meet the company's demands, the family moves. If it is the husband whose job demanded the move, immediately the husband is integrated into a social network at his new place of business. He doesn't feel much loneliness, because he is surrounded by new people and is absorbed in learning how to do well in his new position.

But if the wife does not work outside the home, things may be very different for her. When she has completed the work of decorating the new house she is left to think about the old friends she now misses and about becoming integrated into the new neighborhood. It is just here that she often runs into some serious problems. Researcher Robert Weiss tells us about Mrs. Phillips, "an uprooted woman," who is a good example of the difficulty a woman may have.[2]

Mrs. Phillips, in her late 40s, was a well-balanced woman, gregarious, outgoing, involved in church and general community life. She was a leader in Scouts, enjoyed entertaining in her home and had many friends and acquaintances.

Her husband, a business executive, had an opportunity

for a new position, but the change would mean moving to a distant city. Together they decided to make the move. They bought a large house in a suburb and settled in.

One would have thought that Mrs. Phillips would have no trouble feeling at home in her new location, but there were barriers. They moved in the winter, and cold weather prevented the outdoor activities that bring neighbors together. The couples in the neighborhood were younger than she, and the neighborhood children were younger than her own. There was no church of the Phillips's denomination, so to find their church, they had to go outside the area.

Mrs. Phillips felt that there was no social network for her to join. She tried to hold onto her old neighborhood by writing letters, but that just wasn't enough. Boredom set in. She couldn't sleep at night and began to sleep more and more during the day. She began to pressure her husband by being irritable and unfair. He did his best to help her and was especially patient. But she envied him his business contacts and remained angry with him.

Many women in this kind of bind do not realize that their problems such as sleeplessness and irritability and marital friction have something to do with their loneliness for community life. But Mrs. Phillips gained some insight into her problem. As a result she began an intensive campaign to find a neighborhood where she could be comfortable. She was extremely fortunate in that she not only located such a neighborhood in only two weeks' time, but also had the financial resources to make the move immediately.

In their new location she found all she wanted in a community: neighbors of the right age, a church that met their needs and interesting volunteer work. The relationships within the Phillips family improved dramatically and Mrs. Phillips's personal stability and happiness returned. The symptoms of her loneliness vanished completely.

Mrs. Phillips's case demonstrates the basic need to be part of a community. She represents many thousands of women who suffer from this same problem. Dr. James Dobson, a Christian psychologist and child development expert, believes that the breakdown in community among women in this country is quite serious. He has said:

A hundred years ago, . . . women had babies together, they cooked together, sewed together, washed clothes down at the creek together, went through menopause together, and died together. Aunts, mothers, sisters, grandmothers, and neighbors were always ready, comforting and supporting one another. A natural camaraderie developed between women that provided emotional support and instruction in family living—including a kind of folk wisdom. When a new baby was born, there was somebody there to tell the mother how to raise it. Today, however, homemakers are isolated, not only from their busy husbands, but also from one another. Their relatives are spread across the country and their neighbors have gone back to work. This loneliness is distressing and frightening.[3]

So far as I know, no one is suggesting that women return to the creek to do their laundry. But women's need for women and for community social networks is real. We tend to think that we can make rapid changes in our society without suffering loss, but that has proven to be untrue in many areas.

Dr. David Riesman says that seeing what it is costing them, women may be turning against the American dream of upward mobility: "As self-consciousness grows about the costs of geographical mobility, it is possible to imagine a 'union' of wives and children being formed to set up collective roadblocks against their husbands' mobility."[4] He also says that "among many young, educated people today, there appears to be a great longing for community, and an unwillingness to join organizational networks that will force them to move."[5]

As Mrs. Phillips's story shows, when women lose their community, they are likely to turn to their families for the emotional support that communities were intended to give. This places stress on the marriage. Sociologists Myra Weisman and Eugene Pazkel speak of the loss of daily social contact among a particular group of women and then observe that the loss has "made sharing experiences and ventilating problems more difficult. Thus more emotional demands were put upon the nuclear family, especially the husband."[6]

James Dobson agrees when he says, "This loneliness is disturbing and frightening. . . . It also places *great* stress on the marital relationship, focusing all emotional needs on that one significant partner."[7]

So community-loneliness is a considerable problem to Americans today, and the results are far-reaching.

To fulfill the American dream we have come to believe that we can adapt to anything: rapid revision of our system of morality, loss of God, the abandonment of traditions as old as the human race and of the community which has always supplied many of our emotional needs. When communities functioned well, we did not even realize what they were doing for us. When they began to disappear, we were unaware that anything vital was being lost. Now that we are waking up, we are at a loss to know what to do.

It is as though we sat in a child's coaster wagon, tethered by a rope at the top of a high hill, with a long, winding road before us. Seeing the glittering city of our dreams in the distant valley, we cut the rope (community), and down we flew. We had no doubt that we could handle the road and its curves very well. But as our flight has picked up speed we have discovered that the road holds many hairpin curves that we simply can't negotiate successfully.

Other Hindrances to Community

There are personal things that interrupt community life and effectively shut us away to loneliness. Some of these I have already mentioned. For example, when a divorce takes place or a person is widowed, the social group to which both partners belonged is less accessible than it was before. This is a loss of community. Or one may be a newcomer in a community that doesn't accept outsiders. Ill health can render a person incapable of moving about among friends. Other hindrances may be one's own stand-offishness, satisfaction with one's own small world, or shyness.

Anything that leads to loss of contact with the members of a community can produce the kind of isolation we are talking about.

Communities within a Community

Most people these days live in large metropolitan areas, not small towns. In a small town residents achieve a feeling of closeness and mutual support because of their geographical proximity and their distance from other communities. But in metropolitan areas this is not the case. Here community must be found by becoming part of one or more of the groups that form along the lines of occupation, interests, and culture or ethnicity.

There are many such subcommunities in a city. The school often forms such a community, as do groups of tradesmen, teachers and members of other occupations. Sometimes community forms within one's own block, and yet most often it seems we must put out effort to find the network of people who will be our support system.

The Church as a Community

I cannot speak of the church as a subcommunity. It is far more than that. It is the foundation for much of the true community that exists in a neighborhood, either urban or rural. When it functions well, it is the chief agency by which the Holy Spirit infuses love into a society. Some will find this statement hard to accept because of a distasteful experience with a particular congregation. Instead of openness and warmth they found coldness and a closed door. Yet, overall, it is the church that has borne love and tenderness into society.

The church is not only the place where a lonely person may find God, but it is also the place where he or she can find the best kind of community, that which centers around God. It will provide not only a place to worship and learn, but also fellowship, support in crisis and mutual joy in one another's good fortune.

The church is a loneliness-preventing community for many reasons. First of all, the spiritual, intellectual and emotional life of every true believer converges with the spiritual, intellectual and emotional life of every other true believer at the cross. We are followers of Jesus Christ, and that is strong common ground indeed! Second, its members hold many beliefs in common, beliefs about salvation, personal destiny, prayer, moral values and basic doctrinal issues. We pray together, experience mutual forgiveness and possess the same hopes for the life to come.

When we lose someone who has been close to us, it is the fellow believer who can speak the deepest word of comfort. When the pressures of time, workload or finances make life seem too heavy, it is the brother or sister in Christ who will not only pray for us but pitch in and help carry the load in some substantial way.

Even if differences and petty feelings rise between us, when one needs the loving support of another, these mists dissipate as brothers and sisters fall into each other's arms in love and consolation. The love of which Jesus spoke so extensively in John 15, and of which Paul wrote in 1 Corinthians 13, is not just an abstract idea, but something that a great many Christians put into practice. It is this love that is the basis of Christian community.

Believers know better than any secular group how to bear the burdens of others, how to laugh when another laughs and weep when another weeps. Of all the organizations one might name, the church leads in giving help to those in need. It has been the first to reach out to those in prison, the hungry and the naked. Look about you and carefully analyze the scene, and you will see that the church is in the forefront and the secular helping groups follow behind.

It is the church that has given the standards that make community possible. Matthew 5, 6 and 7 give us the high-water mark of social behavior. The standards contained there enable a group of people to exist as a harmonious whole. Paul tells us in Romans 13:10 that "love does no wrong to a neighbor."

It is difficult for us to appreciate how revolutionary the teaching of Jesus really is. We can hardly imagine how much it has affected all of society, to what degree it has been the salt that makes life among others palatable and helps us to be human beings with whom others can live. Even those members of society who do not profess Christ live far different lives than they would had he never spoken.

One has only to live in a community where the church is central and where it has been functioning in true love for many years to see its effect on how the people there feel and conduct themselves toward each other.

For example, a few years ago a sixteen-year-old boy named Bob fell from a horse and suffered brain damage so severe that he could not speak, eat or do anything else for himself. Doctors agreed that Bob might be helped by a process called "patterning," in which a team of five people move the injured person's arms, legs and head rhythmically in hopes that the brain may relearn some of the movements that it once directed the body to make.

But such a program requires dedicated teams of people, five each hour, five hours a day, seven days a week. For three years the community put forth the loving effort necessary to the task, team members coming faithfully an hour or more each week. Bob made gradual progress until suddenly one day his breathing unaccountably stopped. Everyone felt the loss and shared deeply in the family's grief.

By far the greater number of those who gave their time during those three years were from the body of believers in that area. Genuine, enduring love was demonstrated by the community's Christians. But one doesn't have to look to such extreme cases to see the church at work as a community. Everyday life will provide examples of the kind of love and caring that makes life warm and joyful.

Of course you know that entrance into the life of the church is more than social. The social side of it is certainly important, perhaps more important than we often think. But true membership in the body of Christ comes by establishing a personal relationship with God through Jesus Christ. One might already be a part of the church's social network and enjoying many of its benefits, and yet not know Christ. But when one does become a true believer, the social aspects will mean more and become warmer, richer and even more important than in the past. It will become more evident that the body of Christ is a true community.

Nevertheless, some who read this book will not agree with me about the church, because they have had some experience that has left a bad taste in their mouths. There *are* churches that are cold and uncaring, but stop and think of this: congregations have personalities just as individuals do. The coldness of one or more congregations does not mean that all churches are like that. If a person will search and refuse to become discouraged, he or she will find a congregation that cares about its members in a joyful and loving way. A spiritual community is far too important to exclude from one's life because of a few bad experiences.

How to Become Part of a Community

It is possible to move into a neighborhood, go to work, live within the boundaries of one's own yard, frequent personal haunts for many years, and yet not be known by name to the folk three doors away. I have allowed myself to be caught in exactly that trap. What insurance can one have against such a fate? In many cases the answer lies in one's own hands.

Several times I have mentioned the community in which my family and I presently live. I have said that it is warm and open and that we enjoy many good friends here. But as in any community, some people don't agree. Here and there someone will comment that the town is cold and cliquish. Now, I think they are wrong, but they feel this way because they feel the community has never opened its arms to them.

The difference lies in the way each person enters the community and how he or she lives after entering it. When we moved here twelve years ago, circumstances over which we had no control made the difference for us. I had taken work as a counselor for troubled children and youth. This threw me into immediate contact with families, city officials, law enforcement people, schools, service clubs and agencies and most of the churches. From the beginning I was involved in something that was of the first order of importance to these people: the welfare of their young people. As a result, both Linda and I were immediately and warmly received.

Many times the two of us have looked back and realized

that we inadvertently walked into this community in one of the best ways possible. And we have thought that if we ever move to another location, the first thing we must do is to find some way in which to volunteer service to the community, service that will throw us into direct contact with the area's people. On the surface this may seem selfish, and in one way it is. But we know that we *need* the community with its loving warmth and support. If that is selfish, then so be it. But we would do it for another reason too—it is a part of being Christian. What we receive in love returned is a side benefit of our expression of Christ's love through service to a group of people.

To enter a community and perform some service that it holds to be important does three vital things. One, it makes a Christian witness. Two, it meets a need that exists among the people among whom you will live. And last, it gives entrance to community life.

What kind of service can you give? Do some exploring and find out. Write down the needs that you see about you and that others tell you about. Within the church there may be a need for a teacher, or a youth group may need a sponsor. Perhaps you do well in financial matters and the church needs a treasurer. Would the pastor appreciate someone's making visits on behalf of the church? What about a retirement home? Is there a person there who would appreciate someone's coming to read to him or her? The director of the home can tell you.

What about auxiliary service at the hospital? Are there people who volunteer in the nursery or emergency room? Or there may be a need among families with retarded children, or the school may have a program in which community members come in and listen to children who have problems with their reading. What about foster care, and children's softball teams that need coaches, and children who would be glad to have a friend to help them put a model together? You may feel that you have neither the energy nor the time for such involvement. The choice is yours. But if you want to be a part of a warm and caring community, this is one way to go about it. It boils down to this: if you want to have neighbors, be one. We will talk more about this kind of reaching out in the closing chapter.

Every community has a network of relationships. These are not always clearly visible on the surface, and sometimes it takes a while to discover just what they are and how they work. But to become a part of the life of a people, you must tie into that network somewhere. One contact will lead to another and gradually admit you into the world of community activity and support. Eventually you will be thought of as "one of us," and you will be assimilated into the deeper emotional life of the people.

8

Solitude

"And Jacob was left alone; and a
man wrestled with him until the breaking
of the day."
Genesis 32:24

IN THE EARLY DAYS OF WORLD WAR 2, Nazi Germany tor-
pedoed British commercial shipping in the North Atlantic.
Many young men who were left in the water died in a short
time from exposure.

Kurt Hahn, a German of high principles and a member
of the resistance to the Nazis, left Germany and went to
England to found a boys' school. Hahn believed in meeting
the elements—sun, sky, sea and earth—face to face on their
own terms. So the students in his school were given their
physical training by pitting them against violent wind and
weather, both over rugged terrain and on the face of the sea.

As Hahn read of the deaths in the shipping lanes, he concluded that the other youth of Great Britain needed the
same kind of toughening given his own schoolboys. He believed that if led into social, physical and psychological stress
by competent instructors, young men and women could be

prepared to deal with the hardships of life in general. As a result, along with others he founded a sea school and called it "Outward Bound."

The Outward Bound School now exists in at least fourteen countries, with five schools in the United States: a sea school on Hurricane Island, Maine, a swamp school in Georgia, a lake school in the canoe country of Minnesota, and mountaineering schools both in the Cascades and in the Rocky Mountains. In a standard twenty-six-day course, youth and adults pit themselves against great obstacles, always remembering the Outward Bound motto, "To serve, to strive, and not to yield."

The physical obstacles vary with the school's geographical location, but some of the challenges are the same in every course. Can the patrol pull together as a team in order to survive? How can a way be found through the wilderness? How can one go on when it seems impossible?

Toward the end of the course every student is given the challenge of surviving alone in what is called a *solo*. Isolated on a mountainside or in some other remote place, for three days he or she will not see another face, hear another voice, nor have assistance from anyone. The task at hand is to think, evaluate, write daily diary entries, eat no food, drink plenty of water and stay warm.

The logic behind the solo is that isolation is another form of stress, and that when we face it in limited amounts we can grow from it.

We Need to Be Alone

At first glance this chapter may seem to contradict all else I have said. But in spite of the fact that greatly extended periods of isolation are a bad thing, we do need times when we can be by ourselves. Such times present us with the opportunity to take stock, to pray and simply to feel the calm of quietness soaking into our bones. The ideal life is one lived in the company of others, but with regular times when we can be alone.

Being alone and being lonely are two very different things. It is possible to be in a group, large or small, and feel totally alone. While long-term isolation will almost always produce loneliness, we are able to be by ourselves for substantial periods of time without that result. It is possible to be alone and to feel very good about it for a time. Brief periods away don't give us the feeling that we are abandoned. We know that we are loved and that soon we will be with others again.

Called to Isolation

God calls some to follow him in isolation. In fact, we may be isolated from others specifically for Christ's sake. For example, Jesus pronounced special blessing on those whose lives place them cross-grain to society. "Blessed are you," he said, "when men revile you and persecute you and utter all kinds of evil against you falsely on my account" (Mt 5:11). It is good for us to remember that Jesus had great crowds around him, but that when his teaching became demanding they drew back and left him. Jesus turned to the Twelve and asked a question that is filled with pain, "Do you also wish to go away?" (Jn 6:67). Later on, even the Twelve left him to face his most difficult trial alone.

In totalitarian nations, one's witness may cost all freedom, and the Christian may be plunged into the isolation of prison. Jesus warned that this would happen, and the twentieth century, rather than proving to be a time of enlightenment when people would not persecute others for their beliefs, has joined every other century to place thousands of Christians in prison for the sake of Christ.

It is important to realize that God calls each of us to withdraw from society to some degree for the fulfillment of our devotional lives.

Dealing with Necessary Isolation

Think now of being alone on a long-term basis. How can we respond? We may grow bitter and simply curl up and wither away. Or we may draw on our mental and spiritual resources and actually make life worth living.

An excellent example of triumph in loneliness is a woman named Edith Bone. A British subject born in Budapest, she worked as a surgeon with the Austro-Hungarian forces during World War 1. In 1949 she was sentenced to prison for espionage. The Hungarians believed she was a British spy. In 1950 she was placed in solitary confinement. Being sixty-one years old and having no reason to believe she would ever emerge from prison, Dr. Bone was faced with a great problem. How could she make her remaining years worth living?

Her first solitary cell had a floor of putrid, smelly dirt. Mortar crumbled from the ceiling and masses of spider webs hung low. One wall was coated with fungus and another with a thin sheet of ice. The cell was below ground and completely dark.

How would we have reacted? Perhaps we would have shriveled from the first moment in such a cell, but Edith Bone did not. Immediately she set about to make her life worthwhile. She had only one companion, her own mind, and she determined to make it the best companion possible.

First she decided to enjoy and digest all she had learned in her sixty-one years. She recited poetry, translating it from one language to another, and then wrote new verse in her mind, for she had no writing materials.

Next she decided that in her imagination she would tour all the great European cities in which she had ever lived. She walked by the rivers and past the buildings and monuments, and she called on old friends and acquaintances. She had long conversations with those whom she had known, and later reported that it all seemed very real, so real that she had no lack of companionship.

After her tour of the cities of Europe she decided to return to England, walking all the way. She knew the route and the features of the road well. Walking back and forth in her small cell, marking the distances carefully, she passed the Hungarian border, spent a day in Vienna, climbed the mountains of Vorarlburg and crossed into Switzerland. She visited Paris and Calais, and she finally came to the English Channel.

One hundred times to and fro in her cell made one kilometer. To keep track of the distances she made thirty pellets of bread, ten small ones, ten medium and ten large. Each time she passed her table she laid down one small pellet; then after she had laid down ten small ones, she picked them up and put down one medium pellet. In this way she measured ten kilometers with her thirty pellets, and walked twenty kilometers a day.

When at last given light, she made an abacus of bread and broom straws on which she could calculate to one million. Then she took inventories. How many words in her vocabulary? (27,369 in English.) How many birds could she name? How many trees, cars, flowers, wines, or characters in Dickens?

Finally she hit upon a plan to make up for her lack of writing materials. She made letters from bread, three-eighths of an inch high, four thousand of them, and found that with these she could compose up to sixteen lines of verse at a time.

In order to see out of her cell, Edith wanted a spy hole. So she took weeks to extract thirty-two threads unnoticed from her towels, wove them into a cord, looped the cord around the head of a nail and, wiggling and tugging on it day after day, pulled it from the wall. Then she sharpened it on concrete and drilled a tiny hole through the two-inch oak planking of her cell door.

After two years Dr. Bone was given use of the prison library, and for the next four years she studied geometry, trigonometry and enough Greek to be able to read the *Iliad* in the original language.

In 1956 she was set free by British insurgents and returned to England, believing that her seven years of imprisonment had been not only worth living, but quite profitable.[1]

My hat goes off to Edith Bone. Her determination, her ability to accept her isolation, her powers of concentration, all are amazing. Most of us are not so gifted as this remarkable woman, nor so iron willed. But that does not mean we cannot learn from her. Here was a woman who refused to tread water, though cut off from the whole of humanity. She moved ahead and lived life as fully as she could. She did not allow herself to slip into insanity, self-pity, hatred or depression. She avoided the pitfalls and, more than that, climbed great heights by maintaining and developing God's gifts of life, love and a sound mind. She gave us an example of human courage that is worthy of imitation.

Serving by Waiting

Everett Clapp was a farmer-rancher who died of cancer at the age of forty-five. Clapp was a Christian, and he maintained his faith to the end. According to his son Rodney, Clapp had been an active man, a hard worker with ambition and a thirst for living.

During the last year of his life, Clapp was often immobilized for days on end. "With a needle and tube driven into his thigh . . . [he] could not even turn on his side, much less leave the bed."[2] Here was a once-active man, going where no one could go with him, perhaps feeling that he was marking time, doing nothing while waiting for death.

But after his father's death Rodney wrote, "There were friends and family watching Dad, at least one of whom promised that, if Dad turned away from God, so would he."[3] There is a lesson here for any person living a life of enforced loneliness. Unable to share in normal activities, held immobile by illness or by other constricting circumstances, we are doing more than treading water, marking time; we are also witnessing to the grace of God.

Some Good Things about Isolation

Can we say something positive about being alone? Yes, we can. First of all, being alone gives us time to think, sort out, reflect and know ourselves better. There are dangers, of course, such as distorted thinking through isolation, a turning to sourness and bitterness. Yet it can be an opportunity for reorienting ourselves to life. Aloneness gives us time to know God better. He often speaks through solitude in ways that he does not in the company of others. Some kinds of isolation give us freedom to serve God with less restraint. Paul speaks of this, pointing out that marriage, for example, obligates us to please our mates, while the unmarried person is free to serve God without mixed obligation.

Being alone gives us freedom to do things that we personally enjoy. We may listen to the music that we like with no thought for another's tastes. We may eat the food, wear the clothes, keep the hours, attend the functions, play at the hobbies we like.

Another good thing about being alone is that it is possible to adjust to it. I have seen more than one study which shows that the greatest degree of loneliness is not among the old. It seems that they have accepted being alone as a fact of life, and many of them have made a very successful adjustment, becoming quite happy.

The final good thing about being alone is probably the most important of all. If you have experienced loneliness, you will be able to help others who are alone. More about this shortly.

A Flow of Blessing

Much that is good in this present world has flowed from the lives of men and women who have been isolated from others.

For example, think of Moses. For the first forty years of his life he was in Egypt's grandest company. But for his second forty years he was a shepherd in the desert. For days on end he saw nothing but wilderness and sheep. But it was during this time that God spoke to him from the flaming bush. David is another example. David's preparation for public work came largely while he was tending his father's sheep—a lonely occupation. It was while Jacob was alone that he wrestled with the angel of God, thereby settling some deep issues in his life. And Jesus himself spent a forty-day period alone, praying and confronting Satan.

Paul seems to have spent three years alone between his conversion and the beginning of his public ministry. We could also think of the isolation of Elijah, Amos and John the Baptist. Toward the close of his life, the apostle John was in enforced exile on an island, far from his beloved home. It was there that the Lord gave John the book of Revelation.

We might even wonder if God chose the Hebrews to communicate his message to the world partly because they were a nation of nomadic shepherds. Often under the stars, often alone, they could hear him when he spoke.

A Strand through Time

Early in Scripture there is a vivid strand of God's communicating with those who are isolated. The strand is so noticeable that some Christians have lived lives of retirement in order to hear him speak. The monastic movement has been with us since the third century. Men and women whose names we know, such as Clare, Augustine and Benedict, have vigorously promoted lives separated for prayer. To fulfill this purpose as well as to minister to the poor, to teach and to spread the gospel, various orders were formed, such as the Benedictines, Franciscans, Dominicans, Augustinians, Carmelites, Jesuits, Nuns of the Good Shepherd, Sisters of Charity and Mercy, and the Protestant Episcopal Sisterhood of Saint Mary.

The Reformation was hostile to monasticism, and current Protantism has little part in it. Yet it seems foolish to ignore the fact that some of the deepest devotional literature and some of the most respected names in the annals of Christian witness have flowed from these orders or been intimately connected with them. For example, we spoke in an earlier chapter of Brother Lawrence, the Carmelite lay brother and author of *The Practice of the Presence of God*. Augustine founded a contemplative order. Thomas à Kempis, associated with the Brothers of the Common Life, wrote the best-known book of Christian devotion in the world, *The Imitation of Christ*. And Thomas Aquinas, the greatest theologian of the medieval world, studied with the Benedictines before becoming a Dominican.

I ought to add that for the saints of the church the contemplative life has often also been a life of service, not only in prayer but also in meeting the physical needs of great numbers of people. Withdrawal from society for devotion has meant returning to society to serve. Alfred Lord Tennyson wrote deep words about prayer when he said,

Pray for my soul. More things are wrought by prayer
Than this world dreams of. Wherefore, let thy voice
Rise like a fountain for me night and day.
For what are men better than sheep or goats
That nourish a blind life within the brain,
If, knowing God, they lift not hands of prayer
Both for themselves and those who call them friend?
For so the whole round earth is every way
Bound by gold chains about the feet of God.[4]

If this is so, God only knows what these praying orders have accomplished since New Testament times.

While living alone is not the most desirable thing in terms of human comfort, in the economy of God it may be his purpose. There are those with family obligations who long for time to study the Scripture and other Christian writings. They wish to write letters of consolation and encouragement, but cannot because of other demands. There are some who, if they only had the freedom of living alone, would engage in prayer to a degree that they cannot know in a family setting. If you live alone, you may learn the disciplines that others only dream of. You may walk with a special closeness to the Lord in an intercessory ministry. Loneliness may be your cross, but it may also be your opportunity.

A Purpose

For more than a dozen years I have meditated now and again on Psalm 102, thought by some to be a psalm of David. In David's lifetime he experienced a great deal of isolation. He was a shepherd; then he was hurled into the loneliness of fame and leadership. Soon he was torn from his wife Michal and sent running and hiding as an outlaw. Re-established, he was denied the joys of family intimacy because of rivalry and jealousy. The reconciliation with Michal did not work out well, and his children continued to bring him great sorrow.

If this is his psalm, it is no wonder that it is filled with sad and lonely pictures. To God he said, "Do not hide thy face from me." "My days pass away like smoke . . . my heart is smitten like grass." Symbols of isolation abound. He says that he is like "a vulture of the wilderness," "an owl of the waste places," "a lonely bird on the housetop." He speaks of his enemies, of having been slandered, of his feelings of indignation and anger. And then he makes a most terrible accusation. To God he says, "Thou hast taken me up and thrown me away" (v. 10).

Tears and pain virtually drip from the psalm. This man is in agony. Yet surprisingly he finds some degree of consolation. What is it that consoles him? It is this: no matter what happens to him, God will live forever. The nations will eventually honor God's name, and God will hear the prayer of the destitute. Though he himself is filled with sadness, he has a greater concern than for himself. He is more concerned with the glory of God and God's blessing on generations that have not yet seen the light of day. Of God's permanence he says, "Let this be recorded for a generation to come, so that a people yet unborn may praise the Lord."

His loneliness has done two things. First, it has drawn him closer to God. Second, for three thousand years now, it has directed millions to a consolation deeper than their own apparent abandonment.

You and I are unlikely to console millions. But we *can* be pressed closer to God, and we *can* console a few. To the end of time there will be lonely people. Thousands will wish for a mate but never have one. Divorce will continue as a fact of life. War will leave children without parents and home. Prison will produce confinement and solitude.

What if there were none among God's children who could empathize with the world's feeling of isolation? None to know what it is like, none to say, "I feel it too"? How would the consolation of the gospel be conveyed to lonely people?

If you are lonely, and out of your loneliness you are able to take the hand of a child, or an abandoned person, or one tottering with great age, then you will have done more than if you had built a vast financial empire. I don't know the author of these two verses, but they speak deeply to God's purpose in our loneliness.

They took them all away—my toys—

Not one was left;
They set me here, shorn, stripped of humblest joys,
    Anguished, bereft.

I wondered why. The years have flown.
    Unto my hand
Cling weaker, sadder ones who walk alone—
    I understand.[5]

Something beyond Now

Beyond that, we are not yet home. There is a temporariness to our isolation. Sometimes we act as though all the good we shall ever know is in the present, in the life we live today. But of course that is distinctly non-Christian. The closing words of the Apostles' Creed are "I believe in . . . the resurrection of the body, and the life everlasting." We have some valleys of loneliness through which to pass before we reach the open door of home, but a future life of happiness is a cardinal belief of Christians everywhere.

We don't know if the pavement in heaven is really gold. Those words could be figurative. What we do know is that those who trust and obey Christ will be there. We also know that all causes of isolation will be absent from heaven. Rebellion, hate, resentment, social stratification, geographical distances, lack of empathy, inner reservations, failure to understand another's view, lack of love, arrogance, war and death are forever barred from entering there. Since Scripture seems to indicate that the opposites of all these things will be there in abundance, we must assume that heaven will be filled with intimacy!

The longer I live, the more convinced I am that the joys of life lie in relationships with others. Elton Trueblood, now in his eighties, has written, "As I look back upon the course of my life I realize that my chief wealth has been . . . *friendship*."[6] I believe in compensatory joy. What we have lost of the wealth of friendship in this life will be more than repaid in the life to come, through dear and intimate friends we will know there. I believe that heaven will be a place with a free exchange of love, information, feelings, touch and ideas.

The most blessed picture I can imagine, next to meeting Jesus himself, is of a cottage (I'm not much for mansions) in heaven. The cottage has glowing windows in the subdued light of a heavenly evening. The river of life flows quietly nearby. A soft, green sward surrounds the house and is overspread with the luxurious branches of tall trees, and together they fill the twilight air with a fragrance of restful freshness made even more entrancing by flowers very like honeysuckle climbing the posts of the porch.

Sitting on the lawn and in the house are men, women and children, talking, chuckling, loving one another as only the best of friends can do, knowing that nothing will ever again set any one of them apart from the others.

I admit the picture is a reflection of my own best hopes. But if it seems unheavenly to you, perhaps even saccharine, please understand why it seems heavenly to me. It is a picture of the best I have known here, but with the limitations of sin and mortality removed.

If the setting is inaccurate, of one thing I am certain. There will be no loneliness in heaven, and intimacy will be everywhere. Though we may be called to live alone now, the Christian's heavenly future will bring something far different.

Part Three
Reaching Out

9

Reaching for
a Friend

"Friendship is a thing most necessary to life,
since without friends no one would choose to
live, though possessed of all other advantages."
Aristotle

SEVERAL YEARS AGO THE editors of *Psychology Today* asked
their readers this question: "If someone offered you a pill
that would make it possible for you to live five hundred
years would you take it?"[1] Fascinated by the question, I
began to ask my friends what their answers would be.
There was a wide range of response, but the most sensitive
and insightful was from a friend named Jan. She said, "No.
I wouldn't take it. I don't want to outlive my friends." At
least for Jan, Aristotle was right.

When the British arrived on the shores of Australia in
1788, there were perhaps three hundred thousand people
already living there. A people with high intelligence,
chocolate skin and an intricate but materially primitive
culture, they were believed to have come from India hundreds of years before the British.

Since that time, the indigenous population of Australia

has dwindled to about fifty thousand, most of whom live in the northern sectors of the continent. Some of these retain their rich ancient culture and their nomadic ways. These never farm, but live by hunting, fishing and gathering. Some spurn shelters altogether, living and sleeping in the open with very little clothing.

One of the problems these people face is the cold of Australian winter nights. But they deal with the cold in a very natural way. They huddle with their dogs. The colder the night, the more dogs each person gathers around and over himself. By referring to the number of dogs needed to keep warm, they can talk about the degree of last night's cold. They say, for example, "It was a four-dog night"— very cold!

Life is made up of "four-friend days and nights." The more good friends we have about us, the warmer our lives can be.

Companionship

I am unable to find a common word in the English language that is the exact opposite of *alone* or *lonely*. The opposite of *dark* is *light,* the opposite of *strong* is *weak,* and so on. The language is filled with such opposites, but for *alone* and *lonely* there seems to be none.

On the other hand, we can describe the opposite of being alone. It is "to have companions," *companion* coming from two Latin words, *com,* "with," and *panis,* "bread."[2] Companions were originally people who shared bread. The emotion opposite to loneliness is the one we feel when we have good companions. The usual word for this kind of person is *friend.*

In this chapter we will try to deal with some basic questions about friendship. Why should we want friends? How do friendships form? Where do we go to find friends? How can we overcome the barriers to friendship? What kind of

person makes a good friend? What things destroy friendship?

Why Should We Want Friends?

Some folk have all the friends they need without ever
asking how it is done. They are naturally companionable
people. Others don't feel much need for friendships, while
for some the joys of close relationships have gone undis-
covered. And some have successfully learned to ignore the
pain of loneliness.

Yet friends are worth having. They expand our lives. If a
man has none, he lives in a house with only one room, narrow and confined. If he finds a friend, he has added a room
to his house and has twice the space to live and move. As he
adds other friends, his house becomes larger and larger
until it seems boundless. The single room was unattractive
and the air cold and stale. The many rooms are warm and
the air fresh and invigorating. The one room was dark; the
many are filled with the light of a bright morning.

Of course that isn't the whole story. I realize just as you
do that friendships bring not only new joys, but also new
sorrow and testing. We share our friends' problems as well
as their pleasures. Because we are human, any interaction
between two friends will bring its difficulties, sometimes of
major proportions, and they may hurt us a great deal. In
fact some who have been hurt withdraw and refuse to make
new friends in order to protect themselves from further
pain. But surely that is unfortunate, for the benefits of
human love outweigh the pains! The more we relate to
others, the broader and better our lives.

Henry Drummond, a nineteenth-century Scottish clergy-
man and author, once said that life can be defined as cor-
respondence to one's environment. It takes a little thought
to understand just what he meant. A dead man may lie
in state in a magnificent mansion. To his left is a wind-

ing staircase of walnut, and to his right a fountain of fine marble. On the floor is the most luxuriant of carpets. He rests on a grand catafalque, and above him hangs a large, glittering, crystal chandelier. But he neither sees the warm glow of the hand-rubbed walnut, feels the softness of the carpet, hears the flow of the water, nor sees the prismatic light cast from each pendant of the glorious chandelier. He is totally out of contact with his environment. He is dead.

Our environment is composed of more than an inanimate world, however. It also includes other human beings, and we widen our world, increasing our "aliveness" by becoming more aware of them and reaching out to include them in our lives.

The scientist widens her horizons as she extends her study to yet other parts of the universe. The musician's world becomes broader as more musical forms come within his range of interest. In the same way, as we admit others into our range of love and interest, our world becomes more fascinating and alive.

I have always been a bit distrustful of the "hail-fellow-well-met" who reaches out for new friends so easily. But that may only be jealousy, for as I've grown older I've realized that people who reach out to meet many others, who are willing to leave the shelter of their dens to share life, really have a much better time of it than those who withdraw into a narrow personal world. Perhaps the recluse feels safe in his own little cave. But the more one reaches out, and the more one is liked, the greater his or her personal human resources, security and, certainly, pleasure.

Why should we want friends? Because they are a hedge against loneliness. Because they expand our lives. Because they give us great pleasure and opportunity to be useful, and because they bear to us the image of God.

How Do Friendships Form?

A young couple who had separated from each other came to visit about their problem. As it turned out there were many factors involved, but one was that the young man had no friends outside the marriage. This meant that his wife was the only object of his attention, the only one to whom he could talk about his problems. He was smothering her.

So I suggested to him that he make some friends he could enjoy and thereby take some pressure off his marriage. But he looked rather blank and responded, "I guess I don't know how."

If you feel as he did, that you do not know how to make friends, let me assure you that I am not being flippant when I say that you can do it. You can learn. I do not mean that friendships are formed easily and quickly, but that you possess the resources and can develop the skills necessary for having the friends you need.

How do friendships form? At the outset, please realize that one doesn't simply go out and barge into another's life! If we try this, we will most likely be turned away. There are ways to do things, and barging in, monopolizing another's time and forcing someone into an association are not among those ways.

Friendships form around a third element. This is the first thing to remember.

One night several years ago, my family and I were driving along a country road during a thunderstorm. No rain was falling, but the clouds were boiling and lightning flashes were coming one after another. Suddenly someone said, "Look at that light!" We looked and saw a brightly burning point of light, perhaps twice the apparent size of a star, just beneath the center of the most ferocious-looking cloud. I had never seen anything like it before. As it burned, another point of light formed near it, and a few seconds later the first one disappeared. Then another formed in a straight line with the first two, all three of the lights having been equally spaced.

We were mystified. The kids thought we had seen a UFO, and Linda and I were not certain that we had not. The next day I asked others if they had seen the lights. Several had, and one suggested that I call the airport where a local cloud-seeding operation was based. I followed up on the suggestion and described the experience to the man in charge. He told me that we had seen canisters of a chemical dropped at regular intervals from a plane flying above the thundercloud in order to make it rain. He said that before rain or snow can form, there must be particles in the atmosphere around which the moisture in the air can condense to form droplets. The burning chemical placed those particles in the cloud.

This is a good illustration of how friendships form. Just as there must be some particle in the air around which the water may gather to form a droplet, so there must be some third element present to draw two people together. The element that causes the friendship to coalesce is almost always a common interest. C. S. Lewis observed that if one's only interest is in having a friend, he can never have one; that while the gaze of two lovers is fixed on each other, the gaze of two friends is fixed on a third object by which both are fascinated.[3]

There are many different kinds of interests around which people come together. Some come together around recreational or hobby interests such as hunting, fishing, sewing, books, gardening, collecting and so on. Others coalesce around more serious things such as politics, religion or raising children. But no matter what the interest, it is essential to true friendship's formation and continuation. One interest may bring two people together and then fade as another takes its place. For example, two women may get together because they both admire and own Labrador retrievers. But later they discover that each is a very likable person, that their families are compatible and that they have similar religious views. The focus has changed, but there is still a focus that perpetuates the relationship.

C. S. Lewis pointed out that not all friendships are good, because not all common interests are good.[4] Just as we feel a thrill of joy when we find one who shares our aspirations and highest ambitions, we feel a kind of perverse thrill when we find one who loves the same sins that we tend to love. When we love an evil thing and find another who loves it too, and a friendship coalesces around that thing, we are confirmed and strengthened in that evil. With a sympathetic and agreeing heart nearby, we are less likely to be ashamed of our sin and may become bold to indulge in our weakness quite freely.

Two bent together on gossip confirm each other in slander. Bring two misanthropes or two lechers together and you have a seething pot of putrefaction. If the common interest is getting high or drunk or finding sexual pleasure that should be found only in marriage, one can hardly expect sterling, character-building friendship to be the end product. It is infinitely better for two men to become fast friends because they both love trout streams than because they both hate their wives. When complaints, dissatisfactions or skewed outlooks on life are particles around which friendship coalesces, the relationship will contain the seeds of evil rather than the seeds of good. So friendships are as dangerous as they are beneficial. They should be formed around the right kinds of things. Friends should be chosen with care, gathered around us to complement our lives for good and not for evil.

But the central idea is that friendships form around an interest. Having an interest makes you interesting to others who have the same interest. That fact is worth remembering.

In all this I have neglected to say what must be obvious to everyone, that while common interests bring two people together, the association will be very short unless the two people like each other. That is, each must enjoy the other's way of thinking, the other's disposition and, at least to some degree, his or her outlook on life. We will talk more later about what things help and hinder friendship.

"Well, that leaves me out," some may say, "because I have no interests." If you really have no interest in anything, I must admit that your chance for having friends is greatly diminished. But is it really true that you have no interests? Is there no sport that you care about—even a little? If you care about it a little, couldn't that seed be planted, watered and encouraged to grow until it is at least a mild passion? Have you no business interest or spiritual concerns or causes that excite you? Do you care nothing about travel or collecting something or about some avenue of scientific investigation? Do you have a favorite magazine? If you do, you must be interested in the subject matter it covers.

Probably you do have interests, even if they are in an undeveloped form. If you can decide which of these have the best potential and develop one or more of them, your chances for finding friends will be very much enhanced.

Where Do We Go to Find Friends?
"I've never seen such an unfriendly community!"

"This is a cliquish school. I've been on campus for five weeks now and still feel like an outsider!"

"There's nothing to do in this town. No place to go to meet interesting people!"

These complaints are common. Sometimes they are even justified. But whether justified or not, they point to something quite important. Friendships do not come out of thin air. At the risk of being too obvious, I observe that people are material things and must exist in a material place. Though you may be the most fascinating person in the world, if you are not where others are, you will never have friends. For friendships are not only conceived around a third interest, they are conceived in a place.

Babies always—until recently—were conceived in a womb, and at least to the present, no child has ever lived without having been nurtured in a mother's womb. The Latin word for "womb" is *matrix*. This word has passed unchanged into the English language and is used by industrialists, the makers of phonograph records, machinists, geologists, biologists and mathematicians, each in their own field to mean "something in which something else originates or develops." For the geologist, a matrix is the natural material in which a gem, crystal or fossil is embedded. To the biologist it might mean the tissue at the base of a fingernail from which new fingernail material grows. To the industrialist it is a mold, a die or an engraved stamp. To the phonograph-record producer it is the impression of a record from which all copies are made. Just as babies, castings, records and everything else has a womb, or matrix, in which to be formed, so friendships must have a place to grow. This is important because if we want friendships we must go to places where they can be nourished. Even two people who have the same interests need a place to find each other.

A matrix for friendship is any place where people come together around a common interest. There are many who feel alone, or who feel that their town, campus or community is unfriendly, who would find things much different if they would consciously enter a matrix where friendships are formed.

The most obvious places for friendships to form are our own families, the church, our place of work or study, the local community and the world of recreation. For some the family is the richest place for friends to emerge. The best ties, the deepest intimacies, the most profound feelings often center in parents, brothers and sisters, aunts, uncles, children and spouse. For others this is not so. Yet the family must not be overlooked as a possible matrix, since family members often share similar temperaments, many mutual interests, a common approach to life and a natural devotion to each other.

The church is certainly a friend-creating matrix. The new birth experience makes for strong ties with others who have been reborn. Personal salvation, adoration of God, views about interpretation of the Scriptures, moral outlook and attitudes toward service to humanity—all these provide common interests and powerful bonding agents. And since the church is a cross-section of personality types, interests and tastes, it quite likely can provide the broadest and most complete kinds of friendships.

The working place, the school or university is a place for friendships to form. The office worker learns of fellow workers' interests and tastes, ups and downs, sometimes entering into a sympathetic and supporting role. Men and women often develop outside friendships with coworkers, fishing and hunting, attending plays and concerts, bowling, playing softball or tennis together. The same kinds of things develop in an educational setting.

The local community remains a rich source of friendships. Neighbors often come to like each other very much and enter into strong, lasting, satisfying relationships.

The world of recreation, grown so large because of increased leisure time, presents countless opportunities. It is an especially rich matrix for forming friends because folk enjoy such activities more if they share them with others. Recreation seems to bring similar types and outlooks together.

As an illustration of how entering a recreational world may lead to friendships, let me tell you how it worked for me. For years I had been interested in groups that re-enact historical situations. They research a period of history, including clothing, tools, industry, family life and so on, and then recreate the period in a "living history" situation. For some time I had read about such groups, worked at the skills involved and developed an understanding of the field. But I did this alone, because I knew of no one else in my area with the same interest.

Then one day I came across an item in the local news-paper announcing a gathering of such history enthusiasts. When the day came, I drove the eighty miles to the meeting. I introduced myself to one of the men, shared with him some of my own work, and admitted my lack of group experience and my wish to get to know others. He introduced me to the group members and invited me to their next meeting. I made it a point to go. At that meeting I invited one of the men to come to my home to teach me more. He came and brought a friend.

One day several weeks later, one of these men called me, inviting me to his home to see his work. Now we see each other perhaps once a week and talk on the phone often. Besides that, I genuinely like this man and the other club members. I attend the meetings, pay my dues and take part in club projects. My new friend and I arranged to show a film about our hobby at the local library and announced the showing in the newspaper. About forty men, women and young people came to see it, and out of that group a local club has formed. Now I enjoy researching and re-enacting history more than ever before because of having found others who share my feelings, folk who have turned out to be fascinating, interesting and warm. They have become my friends. Yet, two years ago I did not know a single one of them!

There is probably nothing to prevent you from doing something similar. The steps involved were so clear-cut that they almost provide a formula for making friends. Have an interest and take time to develop it. Find others of like mind and gather up the courage to enter their world. The mutual interest is that "particle in the air" around which the friendship coalesces. The setting in which people come together is the matrix for friendship formation.

The world of recreation is so broad that everyone can enter it. Recreation is simply what we do when we do what we want to do. It may involve fishing, sewing, reading, backpacking, singing, sailing, writing, canoeing, photography, archery, painting or gardening. It may be coin or stamp collecting, knitting, crocheting, quilting or mathematics. It may be service oriented: tutoring, providing food or shelter, fundraising or raising consciousness. One may belong to a political organization, a music club, a ceramics class or a china-painting group. The list is as endless as the list of human interests that brings folk together.

What about Separation from Unbelievers?

Some feel that their friends should all be Christians. But if that is true, how are we to bring others to Christ? Where will opportunity come from? Besides, even non-Christians bear some of the image of God. We are able to learn much that is good from them, and we are able to enjoy them. Even if we did not have the gospel to share with them, they are certainly worth our time in terms of pure enjoyment! I don't believe that the separation for which Scripture calls is a separation from the company and companionship of non-Christian people. It *is* a call for separation from some ways of thinking, from some philosophies and practices, but not from others for whom Christ died. Of course we should not enter into close friendships which draw us away from Christ, but we are far from being limited to that kind of possibility.

Aside from the pure enjoyment of others, friendships

open the door to being a help in time of need. In making and being a friend, as in everything else, Jesus is our example. He had the courage and interest to reach out across conventional lines for his friendships. The disciples were hardly the most religious people in the world when he took them to his side. Though he must have felt the criticism of his peers, he took his place with the almost outcast "people of the land" (Jn 7:49; Mt 9:11-13), and he had no reluctance to be identified with the disreputable woman who washed his feet with tears in the house of Simon the Pharisee (Lk 7:36-50).

Because of the variety they bring to our lives and the opportunity they give us to serve, we are richer when we make a point of associating with people unlike ourselves. When we do, our understandings deepen, our horizons widen and life is more enjoyable.

Overcoming the Reluctance Barrier
Our family has three dogs and a cat. One of the dogs is a female miniature poodle named Bitsy. You can tell from her name and breed that Bitsy is quite small. But she's good company to our girls, certainly more intelligent than the other dogs and, within limits, has a pleasant disposition. On the other hand, Bitsy is a snob.

On a cold winter day the other two dogs—an old cocker spaniel and a young mixed breed—and the cat will huddle together by the step, sleeping in the comfort of each other's warmth. But Bitsy will sit apart and shiver, cold and miserable. If one of the other dogs tries to be friendly, she growls and snaps, absolutely rejecting all their overtures. I'm convinced that she would sit there and die before she would condescend to cuddle.

Why does she do that? Bitsy really seems to believe that she is superior to the others, that they are in a lower caste. Too bad she can't conquer her pride and discover how much the other animals could give her if only she would let them! But I can't force the little poodle to like the other dogs. I've tried to break down her reserve by bringing the others near as I stroke and pet her, hoping she will give in and accept their affection. But she will not be changed.

Many folk are like that, lonely because they will not "condescend to cuddle." They will not reach out in warmth, nor will they allow others to get close to them. Why do human beings do this? Some seem to feel a natural reserve that is perhaps inherited. Or it may be learned; I do not know. Some are afraid to trust others because of a bad experience in the past.

A friend told me about a man in another community who made his young son climb a ladder and then kicked it out from under him. As the boy looked up from the ground in disbelief, his father told him to let that teach him never to trust anyone.

I can't vouch for the truth of the story, but it is certainly true that the world has its share of misanthropes, and that some families provide an atmosphere that does not foster trust and warmth.

For some the problem is not distrusting others, but distrusting oneself. Perhaps one suffers from uncertainty about one's own social graces or feelings that one is not interesting to other people or uneasiness about one's ability to carry on a conversation with a strange person. Embarrassed by long pauses in a conversation when neither can think of anything to say, or fearful of forgetting a name or face, one simply stays to oneself. I know about these kinds of things because I feel them myself. From childhood I have been more comfortable in the reveries of my own mind or absorbed in a good book than I am among people. But I have also been somewhat resentful at the joy of those who mix easily, for I really do enjoy others. So I have consciously tried to grow away from that mentality of fear. I have discovered that if I am not afraid, then my partner in conversation is also at ease. I have found that I can usually enter a conversation and enjoy it very much. For me, sociability has been a matter of gaining confidence.

But there are barriers besides distrust and lack of personal confidence. Some say, "I'm too shy." "I'm too busy." Some folk won't reach out because they are angry. Their anger at life, at others, at systems; their distrust of their neighbors and of the church; their suspicions of the motives of those who make overtures—these form a tragic syndrome that shuts them away into a world of isolation and scowling misery.

I'm convinced that much of our isolation, in fact most of it, is self-imposed. The angry person makes himself so undesirable that others choose to leave him alone and be happy rather than to associate with him and be miserable.

If only those who have been hurt could put their fears away! If only angry people could lay their suspicions to rest! If only they could honestly face up to the trauma or pattern that created the anger in the first place and then let it be dissolved in the love of Christ! If only their shell could be broken and the pent-up desire to love and be loved come flowing out!

Not long ago I read a letter from a mother written to E.T., the fictional "Extra Terrestrial" of Steven Spielberg's movie. This woman has a son who is autistic, but who suddenly broke out of his shell of autism. She tells the story in her letter.

Dear E.T.,

I am Tommy Andonain's mother, and I am writing this letter for him as Tom has never learned to write much more than his first name. Tommy is 20 and autistic, and he prefers his own strange inner world to the real one outside himself. Since he has always enjoyed movies filled with special effects, spacecraft and startling aliens, it was only natural for his parents to take him to see "E.T." In the darkened theater, Tommy came to himself. He screamed, he clapped, he laughed, and then he cried real tears. Autistics do not weep, not for themselves or any others. But Tommy wept, and Tommy talked, nonstop, about E.T. He has seen "E.T." three times now and is prone to touching fingers with others and solemnly repeating, "ouch." E.T. has changed his life. It has made him relate to something beyond himself. It's as though Tommy has also been an alien life form and trying to find his way home, just like E.T.

Ann Andonian
Garden Grove, California[5]

The autistic child is not the only one with a shell to be broken. Many of us have shells to a lesser degree, like ice prisons the shape of our own bodies. We can see out; we can hear the laughter and see others touching. But the ice shell keeps us from sharing their personal warmth, from entering into the world of warmly magnetic relationships.

This shell may be made of distrust or simple reserve; of a past betrayal or of a sense of being unlovely, unworthy, inferior to others; or even of a feeling of superiority. It may be made of sad and lonely years when we were unloved as a child. But in spite of the shell there are feelings bottled up inside. One strong feeling is a yearning to have the warmth that others know. We feel like a child sitting on the porch steps alone while others are playing a game and having a wonderful time. She *wants* to play. She wants to laugh, to run, to be a part, yet something inside won't let her.

But if by chance some small thing teases the child into the game, the ice shell shatters and she becomes as warm as the others. On another day she may freeze herself into another shell, but at least for now this one is gone and life is good!

As with the autistic boy and the little girl on the porch

steps, our shells can be shattered. The blow that does it may be a kind word or a human touch. But whatever the outside blow, it also takes something from inside ourselves. For we can work at shattering the shell from within by daring to love, expressing our feelings, reaching out and feeling the warmth of another. How good it is to see a shell broken! How good to feel our own shell shattered!

It is true that when the shell is gone we become vulnerable. The more deeply we feel and the nearer we draw to others, the more vulnerable we are. Someone toward whom we reach can reject us, slap us either verbally or literally, show disinterest, laugh at us, take advantage of us, misunderstand our intentions or otherwise betray our efforts to be a friend. No balanced person enjoys this kind of treatment. But those who treat us badly will be few. Even if we have been dealt with unfairly in the past, the chances are that if we try again, choosing carefully those whom we approach, we will find friends who are kind and thoughtful. Those who respond positively are well worth the effort and possible pain of rejection by a few.

Besides, everyone has rejections. Yours may have come at a particularly devastating time and with crushing strength. But the chief difference between success and failure in friendship is often that the one who succeeds takes rejections bravely in stride and goes on to try again. The one who fails allows rejection to shut him away again in a world of withdrawal and isolation.

It is true that some have thicker skin, that a rejection may not hurt one so much as it hurts another. Yet a person who is willing to reach out to people in spite of possible pain is almost certain to make satisfying and enduring friendships.

The least we can do is honestly face some very important facts. If you dare to reach out and if you stay with the effort, you will have friends. If you choose to remain separate because of your shyness, your past hurts, your ill feelings toward others or whatever reason, then you are much less likely to have them. It is largely a matter of choice or risk or paying the price. You can face up to the choice, make your decision and then courageously live with the result of the choice you make. If because of inner conflicts you cannot bring yourself to overcome your reluctance, then perhaps a skilled counselor could help you work through your feelings. At whatever cost, life is so much better when we break our shells and reach out!

10

Being
a Friend

"A man that hath friends must shew
himself friendly."
Proverbs 18:24 KJV

LAW TOUCHES MOST HUMAN relationships directly. A father who refuses to support his children can be charged in the courts for his failure. A mother failing to care properly for her child can be charged with neglect. There are laws regulating marriage from the day the license is issued until the close of probate. Law regulates business agreements and employer-employee relationships. But it does not regulate friendships. Two human beings are friends not because they are legally bound to be, but because that is what pleases them.

On the other hand, though there are no written laws governing friendship, there are some unwritten rules that do. In 1979 *Psychology Today* asked readers about friendship.[1] They asked questions such as "How many casual or work friends do you have?" "Are more of your close friends of the same sex as you, or of the opposite sex?" "Do you dislike intensely someone who used to be your friend?" "In an emotional crisis, to whom would you first turn for support and advice?" There were sixty-five questions, to which forty thousand readers responded. An analysis of the responses tells us something about the rules of friendship. Here are some observations gleaned from that survey.

Those who had more close and casual friends than average reported fewer feelings of loneliness.

The trait valued by 89 per cent of the respondents as the most important in a friend was the keeping of confidences. The rule: to be a friend, know how to keep secrets.

The second-place trait, valued by 88 per cent, was loyalty. Loyalty was defined as accepting one's friends even though one may not totally approve of their opinions or behavior. The rule: be a nonjudgmental friend.

The third most important characteristic in a friend was warmth and affection. Of course how this is demonstrated would vary from person to person. And it was in demonstration of affection that a special danger between friends of the opposite sex emerged. *Forty-nine per cent of the respondents had had a friendship turn into a sexual relationship,* and 31 per cent had had sexual intercourse with a friend in the month previous to the report. The rule: be affectionate and warm, but guard against impropriety with friends of the opposite sex.

The activity in which friends were most likely to engage was intimate conversation. In fact, the event that most often changed a casual friendship into a close one was an intimate disclosure about oneself. If after the disclosure the friend continued to accept the newly vulnerable one, then affection deepened and the two became close. The rule: be mutually vulnerable and trusting in close friendships.

In some instances following an intimate disclosure, even though acceptance continued, the one who had made the disclosure felt uneasy and the friendship was never the same again. Obviously one takes a risk when revealing intimate details about oneself.

Another important rule that emerged from the study is that two friends must make time for each other. Sixty-two per cent of the respondents gave this high priority. Failure to take time for one's friend reveals to the other that he or she is not as important as a friend ought to be. A friendship formed during a period when we have more leisure will be threatened if new work commitments interrupt the periods we have become accustomed to spending together. Even if such distractions occur, one must continue to make contacts in order to give assurance that one's feelings have not changed.

Why Do Friendships Die?

One of the questions asked in the survey had to do with the cooling or death of friendships. In order of frequency, these were the reasons given:

"One of us moved."

"I felt my friend betrayed me."

"We discovered that we had very different views on issues that were important to me."

"One of us got married."

"My friend became involved with (or married) someone I didn't like."

"A friend borrowed money from me."

"We took a vacation together."

"One of us had a child."

"One of us became markedly more successful at work."

"I got divorced."

"One of us became much richer."

"I borrowed money from my friend."[2]

These twelve categories could be divided into two sections: change of circumstances and conflict. If we move to a new location, we may become inaccessible to each other. New involvements with marriage or a child may take our time away from old friendships. Divorce is a change in circumstance that results in the loss of friends, often because the friendship was between two couples. One of the two couples breaking up often makes continued friendship nearly impossible.

Sometimes conflict rises between two friends that hinders the old warmth; things such as different points of view, feelings of betrayal, borrowed or loaned money, or the development of some inequality. Personality quirks and differences in opinions become more apparent when people are thrown together under unusual circumstances, such as taking a vacation together.

Usually good friendships are more important than any one conflict that might drive the friends apart. If friends become aware of a difference of opinion that might come between them, it might be a good idea to agree not to discuss the highly charged issue.

Not mentioned in the survey is a rather subtle process that often brings friendships to an end. In many cases friendship will go along for years protected by a mutual reserve about criticism. This reserve is established not only against *voicing* criticism, but also against even *thinking* critical thoughts about one's friend. Friendship, like marriage, is an exercise in continually overlooking the faults of our friend. In order to keep this dam against criticism in good repair, one must place such a high value on the friendship that at a very basic mental level he or she will not entertain unforgiving thoughts. He or she will reject feelings of irritation before they form, or as surely as night follows day the friendship will end.

But there sometimes develops among friends of long standing a feeling that they have a right to express negative opinions about their friend's children, business practices, attitudes, and so on. One may get away with expressing these opinions in some relationships, but not in most. If the behavior of our friends is so far out of line that we cannot live with it, perhaps it is better to go our own way than to try to change our friends.

"But," you may counter, "is it ever right for us as Christians to allow the death of a friendship?" I think it is. There are occasions when the death of friendship is quite painless, and there is no cause for guilt or remorse. If two are drawn together by an interest in fishing for bass, and one of the parties loses that interest, there is no guilt incurred.

If an issue surfaces about which two people disagree, about which both feel with great intensity, and if they find they cannot work through their disagreement, then it is probably best that they go different ways.

There are times when we have no choice in the matter. Our friend becomes angry with us. We ask for forgiveness and he or she will not give it. We can pray about the matter and try to bring about reconciliation, but beyond that it is out of our hands. Perhaps the time will come when we will have the opportunity to express our continued love and good will, but until that time we simply have to bear up under grief and be as pleasant as possible when in the person's presence.

Another rule for continuing friendship: shy away from being an arbiter between your friend and someone else. Do not assume that the relationship can bear the load. If integrity demanded that you rule against your friend, it is likely that you would lose him. Indeed, I lost one of the best friends I ever had by allowing myself to be placed in that position. Let someone else do it and keep your friend!

"What's Wrong with Me?"

"I don't like you at all!" Those are stunning words, especially if they are spoken to us by someone we thought of as a friend. They are even more shocking when not spoken in anger, but in a calm, matter-of-fact way. For then we understand that the person really means it. Though we all have a few among our acquaintances who do dislike us, these few are not a great problem since their dislike is balanced by the people who feel differently.

But it is painfully true that some individuals have trouble making and keeping friends. Perhaps you are such a person. If so, it might be a good idea to ask why. It is at least possible that you have a characteristic that detracts from your ability to *be* a good friend. In order to help us recognize some of these detracting traits, I have listed a few in the following paragraphs.

An excessive spirit of competition. For many of us competition is not the object of friendship. To relax, to be oneself, to be at ease and not strained around my friend—this is what I want. I know that I cannot speak for everyone and that some may actually want another against whom to test their mettle. Personally I like to feel that my friend is my equal or somewhat superior to me, a person to whom I can open my thoughts without fear of ridicule, or reveal my failures without feeling that I will be sneered at or that my friend will somehow rejoice to find me diminished.

An angry spirit. Again I speak personally. It is not pleasant to be around someone who has a compulsion to fix blame for everything that goes wrong. The kind of person I'm thinking about talks a lot about today's shoddy workmanship, incompetence in others, crookedness of public officials, the failure of the church and all the evil motives that inspire others to believe differently than he does.

When we live in an undertone of anger we criticize often, lash out or withdraw. In any case we are left alone: others tend to avoid us in order to avoid pain. Paul says that love seeks to believe the best of every person (1 Cor 13:12 Amplified). One of the expressions of love is the desire to think well and speak well of others.

A reforming spirit. No one wants to be another's spiritual or psychological project. It is the responsibility of pastors to press others to reach for greater heights and to bring their lives into better tune with the gospel. But in a friendship there is not much room for that. In fact, it is the kiss of death. Perhaps that's one good reason pastors are sometimes advised not to make close friends of their parishioners. When they try to be both intimate friend and pastor they lose on both counts, unable to be either pastor or friend.

A nonstop talker. In the best friendships silence is not a problem. It's good to feel at ease without a continual flow of words. But some people talk incessantly. I am acquainted with two couples who used to get together frequently to visit. In each couple, one was a nonstop talker while the partner was very quiet. In one couple the talker was the man, and in the other it was the woman. When they got together the two talkers kept a continuous barrage of words going, and the nontalkers just sat grinning and shaking their heads.

There is nothing malicious in being full of words, but nonstop talkers are frequently eased out of relationships and even out of group meetings such as Bible studies simply because others have no opportunity to share their own feelings and insights. It is a fault worth correcting if one wants friends.

A self-criticizing spirit. Humility is a good trait. But some people put themselves down much too often. In making self-deprecating remarks they may be completely sincere, just expressing how they feel about themselves. On the other hand, some may unconsciously be looking for compliments. No matter what the reason behind the self-criticism, after a short while it is likely to begin to weigh on the spirit of their friends. The friends may actually seek relief by staying away. Again, there is nothing malicious going on here, but this behavior is a serious threat to friendships.

A boastful spirit. Opposite trait, extremely irritating, same result.

We could go on and make the list much longer by mentioning folk who borrow things but don't return them, people who are overly aggressive, easily hurt, overly dependent, overly attached, hypercritical, chronically apologetic, undependable, arrogant or dull, and complainers, exploiters and gossips.

Jesus said, "Whatever you wish that men would do to you, do so to them" (Mt 7:12). This is a solution of love, and of course it is the best solution of all. Thomas Kelly used the words *our claimful selves.* He prayed, "Draw us from our claimful selves and give us Thyself. For in Thy Presence we find the complex becoming simple."[3]

The six undesirable personality traits listed here each have roots somewhere in self-centeredness. The reformer is often power hungry, the excessive talker needs to be at center stage, the competitor must be the best, and the angry person has a vendetta. Boastfulness is often the expression of excessive pride or a cover for personal insecurity. Even the self-criticizing spirit is a spirit turned inward toward its own characteristics and problems.

The Lord Jesus lived an earthly life of utter selflessness. His concern was for others. Though it will take much work on our part to transform these undesirable characteristics into positive, attractive ones, his grace does make it possible. It is good for us to pray, "Draw us from our claimful selves and give us Thyself."

Some Valuable Questions
If you have a friend whom you love very much, it goes without saying that you want the friendship to continue. I suggest that you ask yourself some questions about the relationship in order to help keep it and other relationships alive. Here are the questions.

1. What is this friendship about? What is its purpose? Is it recreational? Is it a friendship that centers around work, around a common cause? Does it exist for the purpose of mutual improvement? Do we get together in order to get away from tension and pressure? What has brought us together?

2. What are the limits of the friendship? Can we talk about serious things, or must we keep it light? What will happen if we disagree on an issue about which one or both of us feel very strongly? What will happen if I offer him or her some personal criticism? If my friend asks me for criticism, should I give it, or will it rupture the relationship? What will happen if my friend criticizes me? Can I take it graciously?

3. What does my friend require of me? If he enjoys things I consider vices, does he expect me to enter into them with him? Does she demand more of my time than I want to give?

4. How much is this friendship worth to me? To what limits should I go to maintain it?

5. How much of myself do I dare reveal to my friend? If she knew my worst failure would she still feel warmly toward me, or is it best that I withhold some information from her view?

6. Will this person ever demand loyalty at the cost of moral and spiritual considerations? What will I do if such a demand is made?

I'm sure you will think of other questions that might be asked of your friendship. I encourage you to ask them and deal honestly with the answers.

More Important Than Rules

When Jesus was asked for the most important commandment, he answered that it is wholehearted love and worship of God. But he added that the second commandment is of equal importance. "You shall love your neighbor as yourself. On these two commandments depend all the law and the prophets" (Mt 22:39-40). With love and wisdom we can be ignorant of the rules of friendship and still be a good friend. We can know the rules perfectly, but without love, all is lost.

In making and being a friend, as in everything else, Jesus is our example. I believe he had a personality that made him attractive to people. He may or may not have been a handsome man, but his manner must have been wonderful to experience. Based as it was on love, personal balance and good judgment, it could not have been otherwise. Thomas Watson, an early Puritan leader, wrote of Jesus, "He was tender without being weak, strong without being coarse, lowly without being servile. He had conviction without fanaticism, holiness without pharisaism, passion without prejudice."[4] The more like him we are, the more attractive we will be to those about us.

Another thing more important than rules is simple pleasantness. Others like to be around a person who gives their lives brightness. Mary Chase summed up the idea years ago in the words of the eccentric character Elwood P. Dowd in her Broadway play *Harvey*. Dowd, talking with a psychiatrist named Chumley, said, "Dr. Chumley, my mother used to say to me, 'In this world Elwood'—she always called me Elwood—she'd say, 'In this world, Elwood, you must be oh, so smart, or oh, so pleasant.' For years I was smart. I recommend pleasant. You may quote me."[5]

I first heard that line delivered nearly twenty years ago and was so impressed by it that I typed it out and placed it on my bulletin board where I would see it nearly every day. I believe pleasantness is enormously important.

Forging Friendships

I have a friend whose hobby is blacksmithing. I've gone to

Allen's garage on a Saturday afternoon and watched him turn simple iron bars into useful tools and ornamental shapes.

He fills his 1901 forge bed with coal and starts the fire in the center of the bed over the air vent. Then he dampens the coal around the edge of the fire. He begins to turn the hand crank on the blower, and the flame leaps to life. Continuing to turn the crank, he places an iron bar in the heat and brings it up to a glowing red. Turning from the forge he lays the glowing iron on the anvil and begins to hammer, drawing it out, perhaps flattening it or shaping it on the swage block, perhaps twisting it into spirals.

On occasion he needs to weld two pieces of iron together. For this to work, the coal must be of a quality that will produce great heat. Having coated the parts to be welded with a mixture of silica sand and iron filings, he lays them side by side in the center of the bed of coals and turns the blower until both pieces are glowing so brilliantly that they look like the sun rising on a clear day. In fact he calls the color "sunshine yellow."

The two pieces must be just the right heat in order for the weld to occur. If they are too cool, little or no bonding will take place. If they are too hot, the pieces will slide off each other when laid on the anvil, and when struck will disappear in showers of sparks under the hammer blows.

Allen learns when the pieces have reached the proper heat by taking their cool ends in his hands and touching the heated ends together while they lie in the bed of coals. If the ends slide off each other, they are too hot. If they are easily drawn apart, they are too cool. But if they stick and are reluctant to separate, the heat is right, and they are ready to be welded.

He doesn't rush but, withdrawing the pieces, he turns to the anvil, lays them in proper position and with moderate blows begins to hammer them together. Sparks fly in every direction from the bright iron, and an amazing thing happens. The dark line that separates the two glowing pieces begins to disappear. After several hammer blows the line is gone altogether. Two pieces of iron have become one.

It is like that between friends. Whether they are husband and wife, parent and child or simply two people who enjoy each other's company, deep friendships don't just happen; they are forged. A truly good relationship that can endure shock and stress is not some sweet little thing whose parts floated together and suddenly locked into place. It was forged into one by the heat of emotion, the flux of tolerance, the hammer blows of adversity on the anvil of mutual admiration and love. Such a relationship is not easy to come by, but it is the most valuable thing in the world.

The Path to Friendship

I believe strongly that if you will do these six things, friendship is a near certainty for you.

1. Examine and develop your interests.
2. Enter the proper matrix, a place or group where there are others of similar mind.
3. Contribute to the life and thought of those in the group.
4. Develop traits that draw people—subdue traits that repel them.
5. Reach out to others.
6. Continue to function as a group member even when you feel the process is taking too long.

If you do these things, then friendships will naturally emerge. Over the years you will be able to forge one or more of those into high-quality relationships that will have depth and last a lifetime.

Many Casual Friends—A Few Close Ones

In this chapter I have advised having many friends, but I

have not meant that you should have many *intimate* friends. No one has many intimate friends, for the conditions necessary for two personalities to merge into intimacy simply don't occur often in a single lifetime.

But having many casual friends not only provides security and a pleasant life with many resources and opportunities for service, it also gives one a wide field from which to develop a few very good, close, enduring, intimate friends.

The importance of intimate relationships comes back to the question of loneliness. It isn't so much the number of friends you have that will determine whether or not you are lonely. Rather, freedom from loneliness depends on whether you have a few in whom you can confide; a few with whom you can open up and share your inner feelings, positive and negative. In fact, it is not too bold to say that if you care very much about someone who also cares for you, you cannot be profoundly lonely.

11

Reaching Out to the Lonely

"Yes, . . . this is how I'm made. It's horrible, isn't it? And you're so beautiful!"
Quasimodo to La Esmeralda in
The Hunchback of Notre Dame *by Victor Hugo*

JOHN MERRICK WAS SHUT away from the human race, from any kind voice, from every warm touch, from all good friendship; not in a cage of iron or in a prison of stone, but in a close cell of misshapenness, in calcified flesh that stank horribly and in its ugliness utterly repelled every eye that ever gazed upon it.

Merrick was born in 1860, was abandoned by his parents in childhood and existed by allowing himself to be displayed as a monster in a side show that traveled around England and Europe. He was billed as "the elephant man."

Now, ninety years and more after his death, Merrick's story is known to many through an award-winning play, a television adaptation of that play and a fine dramatization of his life in a major motion picture.

Merrick himself could never have imagined that his name would become widely known. And indeed it would not have become known but for a London physician, Dr. Frederick Treves. Treves, one of England's leading surgeons, was a man of deep compassion and sensitivity. He was lecturer in anatomy and surgeon at the London Hospital and the London Hospital Medical College on Whitechapel Road. He would eventually become Surgeon-Extraordinary to Queen Victoria and later Sergeant Surgeon to King George V. He carried on his medical practice among the cream of English society, the nobility and the royal family itself. But Frederick Treves never forgot the poor.

One November day in 1884, across the way from the Medical College, Treves saw a large canvas banner stretched across an abandoned storefront. On the canvas was a representation of a horribly malformed man and an invitation to pay to see the unfortunate creature. Treves paid and entered the dark, dusty shop for a private viewing.

He found the misshapen thing covered by a blanket and huddled for warmth over a large brick heated by a small gas flame. At the showman's command the creature stood and dropped the blanket to the floor.

Treves was surprised to see a small man, less than average in height. Later he wrote that the man was the "most disgusting specimen of humanity" he had ever seen.

John Merrick's head was as large in circumference as his waist and hideously malformed. From his brow projected a large mass of bone that almost covered one eye, and from the back hung a bag of spongy skin that looked like brown cauliflower. From his mouth protruded a pink stump of bone, turning his upper lip inside out and preventing his speech from being understood or his mouth from closing. It was this tusk-like projection that suggested to some insensitive mind that Merrick be called the elephant man. Because of these malformations, he was incapable of any facial expression whatever. Though he could weep, he could not smile or in any way express his feelings through his countenance.

His right arm was enormous, the hand a mere paddle, but his left arm and hand were normal and even graceful. A huge sacklike mass hung down his back to midthigh, also covered with the brown cauliflower skin. Hanging from his chest was "a bag of the same repulsive flesh . . . like a dewlap suspended from the neck of a lizard. The lower limbs had the character of the deformed arm, . . . unwieldly, dropsical looking and grossly misshapen."[1]

Because of his terrible deformities, because he could not speak clearly and because of the total revulsion in the face of everyone he met, John Merrick was utterly shy and withdrawn. In addition to the terrible sight he presented to the eyes, a horrible stench rose from the cauliflower skin, making it extremely difficult for others to tolerate his presence. He was an outcast to the greatest degree. Treves later wrote that this "huddled-up figure was the embodiment of loneliness."[2]

When Treves realized the extent of his deformities, his immediate reaction was to hope that Merrick was an imbecile, because then he might not be aware of his own terrible condition. Because of the expressionless face, Treves believed that to be the case. But the sad truth was that Merrick was highly intelligent and very much aware of all the implications of his deformities. Worse yet, he was a romantic at heart, intensely sensitive to the revulsion women felt for him and to his complete separation from his own kind.

Treves's full account is given in the book about Merrick by anthropologist Ashley Montagu, *The Elephant Man: A Study in Human Dignity.*[3] This is the story of an intensely lonely man saved from his loneliness by another man who reached out to him. Treves rescued Merrick from much of his misery and from his degradation, cared for his physical needs in the best way possible, and placed him among people who accepted him and gave him joys he had not before even hoped to know. From a state of utter isolation and misery, Merrick moved into a brighter world. He was able to tell Treves on several occasions, "I am happy every hour of the day."[4]

Others like Him

Most of us have never seen anyone quite like John Merrick. Grossly deformed people are placed in institutions and kept from our view or are medically treated with greater success than in Merrick's day. But such folk do exist.

The purpose of this chapter is not to discuss those who suffer from multiple neurofibromatosis. When I say there are many like Merrick, I don't mean there are a great many human beings with that disease. Thank God, there are not. What I *do* mean is that a great many are cut off from relationships by some characteristic that makes them unattractive—even revolting—to others.

Befriending the Unlovely

My purpose in writing this chapter is threefold. First, I hope to waken your consciousness to the existence and daily pain of those shut away from friendship by some unlovely characteristic. Second, I want to help you identify a few individuals in your own community who are shut away. Last, I want to urge you to clear-cut action in reaching out to one or more such persons.

At first you may think I am urging you to do this in order to end the loneliness of some unfortunate person. And I will indeed be doing that. Jesus told us clearly that we will be judged in regard to whether we have reached out to such people. In Matthew 25:31-46, he speaks of the nations being gathered before him in judgment, and in verses 34 through 36 he says:

Then the King will say to those at his right hand, "Come,

O blessed of my Father, inherit the kingdom prepared for you from the foundation of the world; for I was hungry and you gave me food, I was thirsty and you gave me drink, I was a stranger and you welcomed me, I was naked and you clothed me, I was sick and you visited me, I was in prison and you came to me."

So, just as you suspect, I am encouraging you to do something to end another's loneliness. But this chapter is also a continuation of the book's theme, how *you* might escape *your own* loneliness. What I am now urging you to do is perhaps more effective an antidote for the disease of loneliness than any other I have offered in the entire book.

I hope you will see that there are *two* people in the account of John Merrick's tragedy and success, and therefore two heros: John Merrick, of course, but also Frederick Treves, the man who reached out, the man who could not be lonely!

Opening Our Eyes

Our eyes are often closed to unlovely people. They may be unlovely physically, or unpleasant in the sense that their condition causes us pain. We try to escape pain whenever we can, whether it is our pain or that of another. For example, we avoid hospitals because there people are suffering or hopelessly ill. We stay away from nursing homes for the aged and infirm. We do this not only because we feel awkward in the presence of a suffering person, but also because we do not like to be reminded of our own mortality.

As a result, the hopelessly ill are often cut off from good relationships just when they need them most. This means loneliness. Because they make us uncomfortable, we abandon them just as the world abandoned John Merrick. However, by avoiding the presence and thought of suffering people, we do a terrible thing, very like what the priest and Levite did in Jesus' story of the man beaten and robbed on the Jerusalem-Jericho road (Lk 10:30-37).

In that account both priest and Levite crossed the road in order to stay as far as possible from the beaten man. In this chapter, let's go to the side of the road where the unlovely person is lying. Let us remove our blinders and look him or her full in the face, taking in the bruises, the gashes and the blood. Let us ask why he or she is lonely, and let us be bold enough to touch the victim and to be a friend. In order to do this, we will look at a few categories of people whose condition has removed them from the mainstream of life. We will think about the aged, the retarded, the imprisoned and the physically handicapped; and we will briefly mention a few others.

A Glowing Aura?
The Scriptures indicate that aged people are to be treated with special respect. They have borne the burden and heat of the day, done their work and contributed to society; and they often are worthy of honor. But we should not deceive ourselves about what it really means to grow old, making it something that it is not, casting a glowing aura about it, even calling it "the golden years." Think of what the poet Robert Browning wrote:

Grow old along with me!
The best is yet to be,
The last of life, for which the first was made.[5]

That's noble, a triumph of human spirit that certainly helps one face the rigors of age. Yet there is also an element of self-deception in it.

Did Browning really believe the last years of life are the best, the ones for which the first were made? I understand that some very good things come in the later years. It is good to think of your work being done, of a family successfully raised, of having time to do the things you have always wished to do. It is good to look back and savor the memory of friendships and loves you have known. It is good to have built financial security and to rest in the knowledge that the material needs of the future have been cared for. It is good to take your grandchildren in your arms and to see the children you have raised from infancy doing well and enjoying life. But these things are only one part of growing old, and for many these good things are not there to enjoy.

Growing old also includes the process we call *aging*. Growing is good. Aging can be bad. Aging is the slowing down and eventual failure of body systems. Restoration processes can't keep up with demand, so our skin loses its suppleness and clarity. Muscles lose their tone. Organs begin to fail at their assigned tasks.

Aging is increased confinement. As we rush through time we become less and less free. An older person cannot move about as easily as in youth. The body no longer responds fully to commands. It is somewhat like being placed in a small cell where everything one does is restricted because of space. No one wants to go to jail and be kept in a barred room with cement walls. Neither does anyone want to become a prisoner of his own body.

In youth, if we want company all we have to do is get out of the house and go visit someone. But as we age that becomes less and less possible, until finally, if we have companionship at all, it may be because others come to us. If others do not come, we are plunged into isolation.

Aging is the loss of relationships. The older we become, the more friends we lose to death. One elderly Christian man said to the folk at prayer meeting one night, "I've reached the age at which I have more friends on the other side than I have here."

Aging is one's own movement toward death. Someday one or more of our vital systems will fail beyond remedy, and we will die. Dying is something we do alone. Even if our dearest ones are gathered about us at the moment, they do not follow us. For some this is the ultimate loneliness.

"A Stranger to Myself"

Aging brings another isolation of which we may not have thought. About two years ago I sat visiting with an elderly friend in her nursing-home apartment. She was ninety-four years old at the time, and at this writing she is still living.

Maude is an intelligent woman, her mind still as keen as a razor's edge. She is the acknowledged matriarch of her clan, the object of much love and deep devotion. With her silver hair carefully pinned up, and with a calm strength in her face, she looks every inch the queen that she is.

But the accumulated snows of ninety-four winters lie heavily upon her. Her shoulders stoop forward. Though her eyes retain their fire, it is a faraway fire, as though seen through a mist. Her hearing is dim, almost gone, and she is able to go about only when and where another is willing to take her.

As we sat talking, Maude mused about not having been allowed to die at a reasonable age, and about how time had taken its toll on her body. And then she said something that rings in my ears to this moment. Looking down at her aged body, her words slow, crisp and carefully articulated, she said, "I am a stranger to myself."

I sat there quietly, absorbing what she had said.

These are not the arms that held her babies. These are not the smooth, youthful hands she used to provide comfort and security for the children she raised. These are not the clear eyes that gazed across the vast prairies of the high plains at the approaching storms of sultry summer days long past. This is not the body that stood straight and strong and young beside her husband in the dusty years of drought. This is not the face smiling down from the portrait on the wall. This stranger is simply not the person she knows to be herself!

But Maude does have consolation. She has loving, attentive, respectful friends and family about her. The deepest loneliness comes to the aged when they have neither the self they have always relied on, nor family, nor friends. This is the kind of loneliness in which one's mate is gone and one's children show little concern because of insensitivity, alienation or geographical distance. Isolated from the familiar community; unable to care for oneself; deprived by illness of activities once enjoyed, compelling interests or any meaningful occupation; and broken in spirit—this brings loneliness of the most terrible kind.

Is old age the "best"? "The last . . . for which the first was made"? Perhaps in wisdom. Perhaps in the sense that heaven's borderland has been reached. Perhaps in the fond recollection of old joys. Perhaps in quiet time to ponder the beauties about us. But in terms of freedom to act, a life on this earth to anticipate, freedom from physical pain, these years may not be the best.

Lonely people, unable or not disposed to reach out, need someone to reach out to them. They need a mixture of young and old with whom to keep company; they need the presence of others who are involved in life. But often we shut elderly people out of our sight because of the pain we feel when we see them and the reminder they give of what we are likely to be one day.

Yet we ourselves have much to gain by reaching out to aged people. Being their friend will enrich us. If we are lovers of the past, we can drink in their reflections and learn much. In fact, a conversation with an older friend is a window on yesterday.

By sitting and listening to the reflections of older friends I have heard personal, first-hand accounts of times long gone and have seen those times through their eyes. In my mind I have gone with an elderly friend on a cold, snowy morning to bring lodgepole pine down from the high Rockies with a team and sled. With my grandfather I've played with Indian children on the forested banks of the Red River when Oklahoma was still an Indian territory.

Through my great-grandfather's eyes I've seen the desolation left in Georgia by Sherman's march to the sea. He saw it at the age of five, and I heard him tell of it when he was ninety.

I've walked to school with a young girl along a country road winding through the Missouri hills during the first flush of autumn, hearing through the crisp air the ring of ears hitting the wagon's side as a farmer harvested his corn in the next valley. I've sat with her as she opened her lunch pail at noon in the country school yard and took out a large biscuit filled with fresh butter and molasses—"the good kind," she said.

Reaching out to an older friend gives me a sense of oneness with yesterday just as my children cause me to feel at one with tomorrow—a continuity that lessens loneliness. As a part of the whole cloth of time, with a pattern made up of threads running from the past and into the future, I am not alone.

Older people need us. We need them.

Mentally Handicapped People
Several years ago a man in his early fifties came to visit me. He was an oil-field man, his hands roughened by hard work, his face showing that he had spend much of his life in the outdoors. I had never seen him before.

"Pastor," he said, "my family and I have lived here just a few weeks. I have a bad back and have to go to the Veteran's Hospital for an operation. My daughter is going to drive me to the city. My wife and boy and my daughter's two children will be alone here for a few days, and I was wondering if you would look in on them occasionally to make sure that everything is O.K." I told him I would, and the next morning he and his daughter left. I never saw him again.

The man had told me that his daughter's children were illegitimate, the father unknown. But in fact, I later learned, *he* was the father of his daughter's children. Periodically he would take her away. They would be gone for months at a time, living together in an incestuous relationship. Then they would return and he would take up where he left off. The "back problem" was just a part of the scam necessary to getting away again.

But here is my reason for telling their story. Besides the daughter and her children there were two other victims. the man's wife and their son. Both mother and son were mentally retarded. The woman could function reasonably well but was handicapped to the degree that her husband could easily deceive her. He knew, too, that even if she understood what was really going on, she could not become independent and leave him. She would not free herself from her dependency.

The boy's case was much worse. At the age of twenty-seven he had been in and out of homes for the mentally deficient. He could not count beyond ten nor spell his own name. He could perform some simple tasks quite well and probably would have gotten along acceptably in a sheltered workshop. But his mother would not hear of such an arrangement, for he was all she had.

The problems of mentally handicapped people are great. One does not need to be an expert to be aware of at least some of the suffering that they endure.

Of course there are degrees of retardation. But it is my belief that one has to go a very long way down the intelligence scale before reaching those who are so profoundly retarded that they are unaware of their condition. Those who are aware must also make comparisons between themselves and normal individuals. Many, perhaps most, make the same comparison that Quasimodo made between himself and La Esmeralda. "Yes, . . . this is how I'm made. It's horrible, isn't it? And you're so beautiful!"[6] Imagine the isolation that you would feel when coming to realize that you are profoundly different from others, and how you would feel to be shut out of the mainstream of life.

I once knew a young man and a young woman who met in an institution for mentally handicapped persons. They fell in love and made plans to be married. But their families had a great struggle over the prospect and were finally able to dissuade them. Were the families right in what they did? Could this young couple have coped with the complexities of married life? How would they have cared for children that might have been born to them? Could they have made a living?

Regardless of the wisdom of the marriage, this young couple clearly loved each other very much, had sexual drives that were quite normal and yearned for companionship. These things being true, they were also capable of loneliness just as the rest of us are.

How Do We Reach Out?

We tend to feel more awkward and uncertain with mentally handicapped people than with any other class of people. Yet there are things that can be done to correct our uneasy feelings and to give them a better chance to be part of the human race.

The first thing we can do is to make a conscious choice to include such people in our world. We will lose our fear and awkwardness after a short time and learn to communicate with and think of these folk as people with longings and hopes similar to our own.

Some efforts are being made to receive mentally handicapped people into the activities of normal social life. For example, rather than placing them in special schools, whenever possible they are now being taught in regular classrooms. This is called *mainstreaming* because these children are being brought into the mainstream of life. Of course there are those who cannot function in the normal classroom, but many can.

Substantial efforts are also being made to assist young mentally handicapped adults in establishing an independent life. Some believe that as high as 85 per cent of them can achieve social and vocational independence if given the proper training and support. In some areas they are being encouraged to marry, live outside institutions, and hold regular jobs. One interested group that aids the handicapped calls this "Doing the best we can to help others do the best they can."

In the last few years we have all become aware of the athletic programs for retarded people, the Special Olympics. Such programs require volunteer help from those who care enough to reach out.

Several months ago my wife, Linda, and I visited a local community program for mentally handicapped people. This particular activity took place on a Thursday evening and involved about fifty people in a program called REACH—Religious Education and Activities for the Community Handicapped. Sponsored by the Catholic church the program is carried on with the help of Christian volunteers, both Catholic and Protestant. Its purpose is to give mentally handicapped people in the community an opportunity to study the Scriptures and worship together as a group.

The students ranged from early teens to past middle age, from mildly to severely retarded. As we stepped into the lighted foyer we were met by a group of outgoing, friendly people who made us feel at home immediately. They had none of the reserve that keep many adults from making friends quickly, and they gave us such an enthusiastic welcome that we were certain they really were glad we had come.

During the Bible study, class members answered questions about Scripture and the Christian life. In worship they were reverent. Several led in prayer, freely telling God what they wanted, expressing themselves easily, thanking him openly. When the study and prayer time was over I knew I had worshiped with brothers and sisters in Christ as surely as if I had been in a service with the most learned people.

But these folk live hard lives. Their families have had years of profound sorrow at the handicaps their children bear. Their childish simplicity and openness must weary family members and teachers, and I expect it often brings down wrath and expressions of exasperation. Their exuberance must be a great cross at times.

Knowing that one is apart because of imperfect physical development, that others can never, no matter how hard they try, enter one's own world with all its special feelings and perceptions, must bring a great sense of loneliness to many retarded people. Their greatest need, apart from physical care, is for someone who will reach out to them, who will love them with understanding and with the same open, free sincerity with which they love.

Prisoners
A man awaiting trial for murder was being held in our county. I remember seeing him behind the high chain-link fence just outside the jail, soaking up his weekly allowance of sun. In a few months he was found guilty of murder in the first degree and sentenced to life in prison. His crime was made especially repulsive by the fact that he had forced his own young daughter to assist him in the killing.

But the thing I remember most was what I saw at that chain-link fence. Knowing that he would be there on certain days, his wife would come to see him. I recall how they touched each other through the openings in the heavy wire, how they pressed their bodies hard against that barrier in a desperate effort to simulate an embrace. I remember how she wept, and how pitifully puzzled and ashamed their little girls appeared to be.

No matter what a person has done, he or she needs someone to be close to. The punishment may be just, but no one should be left utterly alone. After all, Christ has given us the joy of his presence in spite of our own sin.

This imprisoned man's wife and children needed the warm touch of Christian people as much as he. They were shut out of society as surely as he was, in spite of the fact that he was the one who had committed the crime. They were outcasts by association, faced with making a living in a community where the man's crime was known to all. They were faced with the emotional pressures and adjustments of a future of separation from husband and father.

It is difficult to go to a prison. A visit through a thick glass window and a wire grate is terribly unsatisfying, and the noise in the visiting room is so distracting that it seems almost impossible to carry on a serious conversation. And who knows just what to say to a person behind bars? Besides, the helper is so vulnerable. The guilty person may try to con his or her new friend in many ways. He or she may ask for favors and make requests that are difficult to respond to. On some occasions there may even be a threat to one's property or life itself. Yet are these not the risks that one must take in order to follow Christ?

A Christian woman visited the women's section of the county jail in her city. She went because she had read the words of Jesus, "I was in prison and you came to me" (Mt 25:36).

She was struck by the bare floors, the bleak walls and the barred windows, and by the women themselves, women whose worn faces reflected the hard lives they had lived. There were prostitutes, alcoholics and drug addicts as well as one girl who was a first-time offender, unmarried and pregnant.

The visitor was permitted to lead the women in a Bible study and bring them food and good reading material. She was also able to help the pregnant girl. She learned that the girl's father had forced her into incest. She prayed with her and helped her consider the options for her own and her baby's future. Step by step she saw her through her pregnancy and prison term.

This woman could not do everything, but she did what she could, and she did it in faithful obedience to Christ. She was finding someone to love, someone who was—at least on the surface—quite unlovely. She was not only obeying, she was modeling her behavior after the Lord's, for we see in Romans 5:6-8 how he loves the unlovely:

> While we were still weak, at the right time Christ died for the ungodly. Why, one will hardly die for a righteous man—though perhaps for a good man one will dare even to die. But God shows his love for us in that while we were yet sinners Christ died for us.

Physically Handicapped People

We may not think of physically handicapped people as lonely. Many undoubtedly are not. But some handicaps create special opportunities for loneliness. Think of the boy with a physical disability sitting on the sidelines watching the other fellows play football, or the girl who would like more than anything to be on the girls' basketball team, but who has a heart defect that will not permit vigorous activity.

Recently I saw the old movie *The Miracle Worker*, the story of Anne Sullivan's work with young Helen Keller. Helen

Keller was blind and deaf from the age of nineteen months, the only avenues of communication left to her were touch, smell and taste. It is hard to imagine such intense deprivation. Yet at the age of sixteen she entered the Cambridge School for Young Ladies, and at twenty, Radcliffe College —both schools for the hearing and sighted. After four years of study she graduated from Radcliffe cum laude. Afterward she became a writer and lecturer, traveled widely and championed causes of the handicapped. She has long been considered one of the great women of the world.

The accomplishments of Helen Keller amaze me. That anyone so thoroughly deprived of normal input could attain such a degree of understanding leaves me in awe. But I am no less in awe of Anne Sullivan! She began at the age of twenty to teach seven-year-old Helen. She met the child at least halfway in this forest of deprivation, clearing and paving a road to lead her out of her darkness. When sixteen-year-old Helen went to school, Anne Sullivan went with her, attending classes and translating every lecture to Helen by touch. She did the same at Radcliffe. For forty-nine years, until the time of Anne Sullivan's death in 1936, she was Helen Keller's contact with the world.

As with Frederick Treves and John Merrick, the triumph belonged to two people, not just one. One was shut away until the other came to help. One reached in and the other reached out.

I have a dear friend who lives with his wife and children in Portland, Oregon. We met in high school. I had just moved into the community to attend the church-related school. He took me, the newcomer, under his wing and made me feel at home. We had many long hours of conversation; we prayed together alongside running streams, in dormitory rooms and on the tops of high hills. When school days were done we went our separate ways, each to small pastoral charges, and then for several years we lost contact.

The time came when I needed him and sought him out again. Once more we enjoyed a fellowship similar to the one we had known before.

In the time we had been apart, he and his wife had opened their home to foster children, and in one year alone over two hundred children, ranging from infancy to late teens, had found shelter there. In addition to having two biological children, over a period of time they adopted two sets of twins. Cliff and Muriel were not wealthy people, but they were always reaching out to somebody who needed them. In all this they continued the normal work of pastoral ministry. Cliff also established a police chaplaincy in a city of over a hundred thousand, entering daily into the trauma of crisis intervention.

But about two years ago, Cliff reached a point of personal crisis. He discovered he was rapidly losing all his hearing. You can imagine how this active, outgoing man must have felt. From a world of silence, how could he continue to reach out as a pastor, foster parent or police chaplain?

Rather than give up his public service for Christ, Cliff and his family moved to Portland, where he entered a special seminary program that would train him to minister to the deaf. Out of his increasing silence he is reaching out to others who live in that same world, reaching out to alleviate loneliness, to lift burdens, to bring others to Christ. I think my friend is the most successful man I have ever known.

I have used deafness as only one example of physical limitation that can shut a person out, but there are many other such limitations. Blindness comes quickly to mind. Whatever the problem, in each case you and I can take steps toward understanding it more clearly. The better we understand, the more likely the Lord can show us a path toward the person who is lonely.

I have a friend whose younger brother was born without hearing. Recently he and his wife attended the local junior college in the evenings to take a course in sign language. Now when the family gets together they are able to communicate much more clearly with his brother and actually bring him into the conversations. Imagine the difference that makes.

Many Others

There are many things other than age, retardation, imprisonment and physical handicap that can shut people out of the mainstream of society. We all know someone who has a character quirk, some irritating arrogance, some strange manner that drives others away.

There are the mentally ill people, shunted aside because we don't understand mental illness or because the person is a physical threat. Embittered people are often isolated. Looking at life through grimy, streaked windows, they see everything in its worst light, and everyone is blameworthy in their eyes. This kind of person is easy to shun since he or she casts such a shadow on the side of the road. But what would Jesus do? A friend might make a difference.

There are also children without fathers, and teen-agers who are consummately alone—in the view of some sociologists and psychologists, the loneliest of all groups. There are depressed people, unemployed people, college students away from home, youngsters in trouble with the law, newcomers to the community, schoolchildren who cannot keep up with their classmates, those who are dying. There are many candidates for your friendship. Sometimes I think that every person we meet is fighting a hard battle and that warm affection from the right person could make the crucial difference. Christ makes himself known to others as their friend only as we reach out.

Breaking the Tether

Unfortunately we don't reach out nearly enough. Something holds us back, something like a tether. We are tethered by preoccupation with our own domain. In an egocentric way, taken up with our own world, we wish to be left alone to go our way uninterrupted. But preoccupation that excludes others is sin and, because it is sin, it is to be repented of.

Another tether is vanity. We don't reach out because we don't want to be associated with someone of a certain financial, social or intellectual level. Sometimes we are actually afraid to be a friend to someone because the association will "spoil our image." Of course this is sin.

Sometimes we are tethered because we fear the emotional impact lonely people would have on us. "It depresses me to go to the nursing home and see all those old people." "I want to be a comfort to her, but I'll just cry when I see how sad she is." I recall vividly the day the sheriff brought me two little girls left without home or parents. Beautiful children, they were so bewildered and afraid I had to leave the room to weep.

Another tether that holds us back is a lack of confidence in our ability to help. Twenty-four years ago, as a student pastor in a rural congregation, I was horrified by crisis situations. When one of the families in the community lost a little boy by accidental hanging, I could not make myself go to the home to express my sorrow. They were faithful members of another congregation and therefore not my pastoral responsibility, but my predominant reason for not going was that I just didn't know what to do to help and had no idea of what I should say to them.

But one of my church leaders came to me and said, "You've got to go." When I told him how terrified I was and that I had no idea what to say, he said, "Just tell them how sorry you are." There was a world of wisdom in that advice.

We all have the ability to listen sympathetically. Most people are emotionally free enough to slip an arm around someone who is hurting or at least to give a tight, lingering handclasp that says, "I care." There is no need to have all the answers. Being present, warm and caring is the best thing that can be done in many situations. Making another's burden our own, feeling and weeping with them, is a vital part of burden bearing. The Scripture says, "Weep with those who weep" (Rom 12:15).

The last tether I will mention is fear that someone will take advantage of us. And they may. The possibility is certainly real. Some folk you try to reach will begin to feel that you owe them the service you are giving and will begin to use you. Your car is now their taxi, a sack of groceries is due every week, they continually interrupt the time that belongs to your family, they come over to weep on your shoulder, and they keep you up late night after night.

It is true that we must know when to say "no" or "wait." Wisdom and compassion are necessary for balance. But at the same time we must remember whom we are following. People took advantage of Jesus, and as his disciples we must be willing to take the risk.

A Place to Stand

A decade and a half ago, Elton Trueblood wrote a book to which he gave the title *A Place to Stand*. In it he quoted Archimedes' famous observation about leverage, "Give me a place to stand and I will move the earth." Trueblood dedicated the book to the founder of a great pharmaceutical company, a man who gave large amounts of money to foundations and to those in need. The dedication reads: "To Eli Lilly who, because he has found a place to stand, has been able to lift many burdens."[7]

The best kind of reaching out is done when the person who is reaching is also standing on firm ground. A man mired in quicksand cannot lift another man out. Those who wish to help others out of loneliness must have their feet planted on Christ.

The more attention we give to others, the less concern and pity we have for ourselves. When we invest in the welfare of someone else we find peace, rest, fulfillment and pleasure. Perhaps this is partly what Jesus was trying to tell us when he said, "For whoever would save his life will lose it; and whoever loses his life for my sake and the gospel's will save it" (Mk 8:35).

Service to others also relieves our loneliness. Ecclesiastes 11:1 says, "Cast your bread upon the waters, for you will find it after many days." Proverbs 19:17 tells us, "He who is kind to the poor lends to the LORD, and he will repay him for his deed."

Service is a solution to loneliness because Jesus becomes increasingly real to those who reach out. Inward ecstasy is fine, but it is only part of knowing Christ. His words in Matthew 25:31-46 indicate that Jesus regards our behavior toward others as behavior toward himself. This is profound and important! The great saints of the past and present have emphasized both the inner devotional life and the life of service. Think of Francis of Assisi, Brother Lawrence, John Wesley, John Woolman and Mother Teresa.

When we serve, some kinds of loneliness fade into the background of our attention and bother us much less. Other kinds are banished altogether.

Finding Someone to Love

Many years ago Russ Morgan wrote a song which became very popular. It dealt in an unusual way with the topic of love: "You're nobody till somebody loves you. You're nobody till somebody cares." Those lyrics would lead us to believe that the most important thing in life is to find somebody to love you. But Morgan was trying to say something very different. He revealed his message at the end with the surprise line, "So find yourself somebody to love!" That is exactly the conclusion that you and I have reached. Don't wait for someone to come to you. You may have to wait a long time. Take the initiative and erase your own loneliness by finding somebody to love.

In the process of writing this book I made a discovery that I had not anticipated at all. I expect it to make a permanent difference in my life and thought. It is this: nothing is more important than relationships. Even truth itself, vital as it is, is important because it serves relationships. In Jesus' parables about the three lost things—a sheep, a coin and a son—we see the value God places on one who is away from him and the warmth with which he receives one who returns (Lk 15).

In Victor Hugo's *The Hunchback of Notre Dame,* only one person loved fully. It was not the corrupt archdeacon, nor the vain captain, nor even La Esmeralda, though she gave water to Quasimodo when he was chained to the pillory. It was Quasimodo himself. He had no form nor comeliness that La Esmeralda should desire him, but to the end he gave his life in order to be near her. Christ has done the same for us. His sacrifice was made for the purpose of reconciliation; put another way, his sacrifice was made to restore relationships.

We ought to live every day with relationships as our highest priority. They are absolutely necessary. That is the reason loneliness is such a terrible emotion.

The Warmth of Spring
I am writing this page on a strangely dreary day. The month of March is almost gone, yet snow has covered the prairies for many days now. The gray sky is heavily overcast and misty, silver fog sweeps across the countryside. The wind is blowing strongly from the south, rattling the door and moaning around the eaves of my study. The snow is melting before the wind, but the glass remains low. The

wind will continue into the night, the temperature will drop again toward evening and new snow will begin to fall.

If this were November, we would be glad for the promised storm. The new and different world of ice and snow would be a happy change after the months of heat. We would welcome the white solitude by warming our houses, popping corn, playing games and feeling the exhilaration of the changing season.

But this is not November. It's March, and we have been shut in by the cold and impeded by drifting snow for too long. Too often the roads to school and to the homes of others and to town have been blocked. We want out! We want to be warm again and free to come and go at will, unhampered by heavy coats and clumsy mittens.

Tonight the storm may come, shutting us away for a few more days. Yet, if it does, we will continue to wait. We will be uneasy, anxious; but we will wait with confidence. Though winter has been long, the snow will disappear before the clearing skies and warming days. We will shed the wraps that kept us warm and walk abroad again in the rays of the springtime sun. The early mornings will be wet with the dew of heaven. The grass will grow luxuriantly over the prairie and the voice of the meadowlark will ring out in all its sweetness. The days will seem as fresh and gloriously full of life as when we were children.

In the same way, though locked in the arctic cold of a winter of loneliness, the chilled heart can know the spring of warm love again. Amid all the intricacy and detail of how one does it, the heart of the matter will always remain, "Find somebody to love."

Notes

Chapter 1: What Is Loneliness?
[1]Richard E. Byrd, *Alone* (New York: G. P. Putnam's Sons, 1938).
[2]Robert S. Weiss, *Loneliness: The Experience of Emotional and Social Isolation* (Cambridge, Mass.: MIT Press, 1973), p. 24.
[3]Ibid., p. 17.
[4]Ibid., pp. 14-15.

Chapter 2: The Dangers of Loneliness
[1]Will Durant and Ariel Durant, *The Story of Civilization*, Vol. 2 (New York: Simon and Schuster, 1954), p. 53.
[2]Maggie Scarf, "The Promiscuous Woman," *Psychology Today* 14, no. 2 (July 1980): 83.
[3]Ibid.

Chapter 3: God
[1]John Houseman, "The Men from Mars," in *Life in Society,* ed. Thomas E. Lasswell et al. (Chicago: Scott, Foresman, 1965), p. 222.
[2]Francis Schaeffer, *He Is There and He Is Not Silent* (Wheaton, Ill.: Tyndale House, 1972).
[3]Frank S. Mead, *The Encyclopedia of Religious Quotations* (Westwood, N.J.: Fleming Revell, 1955), p. 189.
[4]C. S. Lewis quoted in Sherwood Wirt, *Not Me God* (New York: Harper & Row, 1966), p. 7.

[5]James Weldon Johnson, *God's Trombones* (New York: Viking Press, 1927).

[6]C. S. Lewis suggests something similar in *The Problem of Pain* (New York: Macmillan, 1959), pp. 38-39.

[7]Brother Lawrence, *The Practice of the Presence of God* (Old Tappan, N.J.: Fleming Revell, Spire Books, 1958).

[8]Ibid., p. 35.

[9]Ibid., p. 54.

[10]Mead, *Encyclopedia of Religious Quotations*, p. 166.

[11]Lawrence, *Practice of the Presence of God*, p. 29.

[12]Mary Brown Parlee, "The Friendship Bond," *Psychology Today* 13, no. 4 (October 1979): 43.

Chapter 4: Family

[1]"News from the World of Medicine," *Reader's Digest* 111, no. 668 (December 1977): 78.

[2]A. H. Maslow and Bela Mittelmann, *Principles of Abnormal Psychology* (New York: Harper, 1951), pp. 309-18.

[3]Weiss, *Loneliness*, p. 197.

[4]Ibid., p. 51.

[5]Urie Bronfenbrenner and Susan Byrne, "Nobody Home: The Erosion of the American Family," *Psychology Today* 10, no. 12 (May 1977): 41.

[6]Louise Bernikow, *New York Times*, 15 August 1982.

[7]Margaret Sangster, "A Memory Can't Be Bought," *Reader's Digest* 82, no. 489 (January 1963): 113-15.

[8]Weiss, *Loneliness*, p. 231.

Chapter 5: Mate

[1]Michael Demarest, "Platform for Singles," *Time* 118, no. 20 (16 November 1981): 103.

[2]Amitai Etzioni, *An Immodest Agenda: Rebuilding America before the Twenty-First Century* (New York: McGraw Hill, 1982).

[3]Alvin P. Sanoff, "Nineteen Million Singles, Their Joys and Frustrations," *U.S. News and World Report* 94, no. 7 (21 February 1983): 54.

[4]Demarest, "Platform for Singles," *Time*, p. 103.

[5]Weiss, *Loneliness*, p. 233.

[6]Ibid.

[7]Demarest, "Platform for Singles," *Time*, p. 103.

[8]Durant and Durant, *The Story of Civilization*.

[9]Demarest, "Platform for Singles," *Time*, p. 103.

[10]Weiss, *Loneliness*, pp. 62-66.

[11]C. S. Lewis, *A Grief Observed* (New York: Bantam Books, 1976), p. 147.

[12]Ibid., pp. 147-48.

[13]Ibid., p. 20.

Chapter 6: Intimacy and Romance

[1]Jeanne Hendricks, *A Woman for All Seasons* (Nashville: Thomas Nelson, 1977).

[2]Louise Bernikow, *New York Times*, 15 August 1982.

[3]Perry London, "The Intimacy Gap," *Psychology Today* 11, no. 11 (May 1978): 45.

[4]Hannah Lee, *Help Your Husband Stay Alive* (New York: Appleton-Century Crofts, n.d.).

Chapter 7: Community

[1]*Rand McNally Road Atlas* (Chicago: Rand McNally, 1981).

[2]Weiss, *Loneliness*, p. 165.

[3]James Dobson, interview, *Christianity Today* 16, no. 9 (7 May 1982): 16.

[4]Quoted in Weiss, *Loneliness*, p. xiii.

[5]Ibid., p. xvi.

[6]Ibid., p. 160.

[7]Dobson, *Christianity Today*, p. 16.

Chapter 8: Solitude

[1]Edith Bone, *Seven Years Solitary* (New York: Harcourt, Brace and Company, 1957).

[2]Rodney Clapp, "Dying Was a Way of Life," *Christianity Today* 27, no. 6 (18 March 1983): 12.

[3]Ibid., p. 63.

[4]Alfred Lord Tennyson, "Idylls of the King: The Passing of Arthur," in *The Poetic and Dramatic Works of Alfred Lord Tennyson* (Boston: Houghton Mifflin, 1898), p. 449.

[5]V. Raymond Edman, *The Disciplines of Life* (Wheaton, Ill.: Scripture Press, 1948), p. 119.

[6]D. Elton Trueblood, *Essays in Gratitude* (Nashville: Broadman Press, 1983).

Chapter 9: Reaching for a Friend

[1]"Who Wants to Live Five Hundred Years? Men Do," *Psychology Today* 17, no. 3 (March 1983): 81.

[2]"Picturesque Word Origins," *Webster's New International Dictionary* (Springfield, Mass.: G. & C. Merriam, 1933), p. 47.

[3]C. S. Lewis, *The Four Loves* (New York: Harcourt Brace Jovanovich, 1960), pp. 91, 98.

[4]Ibid., p. 113.

[5]"A Letter to E.T.," *People Weekly* 18, no. 26 (3 January 1983): 71.

Chapter 10: Being a Friend

[1]"Friendship: An Inquiry," *Psychology Today* 12, no. 10 (March 1979): 69.

[2]Ibid., p. 50.

[3]Thomas Kelly, _A Testament of Devotion_ (Nashville: The Upper Room, 1955), p. 15.

[4]Walter B. Knight, _Knight's Illustrations for Today_ (Chicago: Moody Press, 1980), p. 170.

[5]Mary Chase, _Harvey,_ Best American Plays (New York: Crown Publishers, 1970), p. 603.

Chapter 11: Reaching Out to the Lonely

[1]Ashley Montagu, _The Elephant Man: A Study in Human Dignity_ (New York: E. P. Dutton, 1979), p. 16.

[2]Ibid., p. 14.

[3]Ibid.

[4]Ibid., p. 29.

[5]Robert Browning, "Rabbi Ben Ezra," _Dramatis Personae,_ Stanza I.

[6]Victor Hugo, _The Hunchback of Notre Dame_ (New York: Bantam Books, 1963), p. 186.

[7]D. Elton Trueblood, _A Place to Stand_ (New York: Harper & Row, 1969), p. 5.